THE LONELIEST GAME

The Loneliest Game

A Play in 3 Acts

by

Paul T. Nolan

with an Introduction

by Jane F. Bonin

Edgemoor Publishing Company
Houston, Texas

Library of Congress Catalog Card Number: 73-93779

ISBN: 0-88204-003-0

Winner of the National Workshop Players Award

Listed in BEST AMERICAN PLAYS 1964-65

Analyzed in PRIZE-WINNING AMERICAN DRAMA, 1973

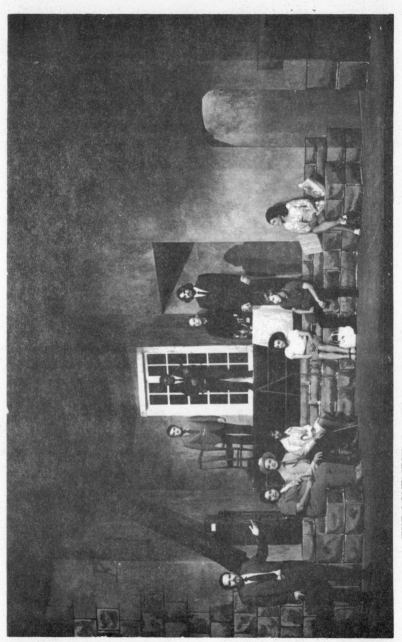

THE LONELIEST GAME was produced by the University of Southwestern Louisiana players July 21-25, 1971, with a modified thrust stage. This was the

The "death-makers" of THE LONELIEST GAME in an opening scene from the 1971 production of the play, done by the University of Southwestern Louisiana.

Time: Now

Place: The entire action takes place in the Gates living room of his island house, on a small rock somewhere off the coast of the United States.

CHARACTERS

THE DEATH-MAKERS:

    MR. GATES, the host

    MRS. CLYME, the housekeeper

    DONNE, first assistant

    MUTE, second assistant

THE LONELY:

    MISS BRITT, a middle-aged spinster

    SABRE DAWSON, a career woman

    FAYE ALLEN, a run-away wife

    DUKE TAYLOR, an itinerant worker

    MR. ROGERS, a bachelor

    LORETTA GRANT, a Negro school teacher

    BILLY JOE JENKINS, a Southerner

THE SET

The living room of the Gates home is a large, high-ceilinged box, the central room of a rambling house somewhere off the coast of the United States. A staircase on the right of the back wall rises to a small balcony with a door leading to the sleeping quarters. Beneath the balcony, in the center of the up-stage wall, are double doors that lead to the main entrance of the house, on the island side. The door is set back under the balcony so that one standing on the balcony cannot see the door. The section between the balcony and the door is a bookcase, filled with books having something to do with loneli-ness — THE LONELY CROWD, ROBINSON CRUSOE, etc. The left wall is almost completely taken up with French doors, opening on a patio that overlooks a roaring, rock-dotted sea, a hundred or so feet below the patio. When the doors are open, the sea can be heard. Along the right wall is a long sofa, at each end of which is a small table. In the center of the room, downstage from the bal-cony, is another sofa, a coffee table before it, with other chairs flanking the table. Out from the French doors are occasional chairs and tables. In spite of the spaciousness of the room, there is an air of loneliness, de-pression, and even poverty about the scene.

SYNOPSIS

ACT ONE

INTRODUCTION

Paul T. Nolan, a prolific and versatile writer, has published over two hundred books, plays, and articles for an audience of scholars and critics, teachers and students, literate nonspecialists, and those with popular tastes as well. In spite of his numerous publications, however, Nolan, presently the Dupre Professor of Humanities at the University of Southwestern Louisiana, thinks of himself as a teacher who writes rather than a writer who teaches. In a study of Nolan's work, *The Teacher as Writer: Paul T. Nolan, Example,* 1970, James M. Salem suggests that for Nolan, the printed page and the stage are extensions of the classroom. His work as a playwright, for example, has been done primarily for the nonprofessional stage. In fact, of the eighty-one plays listed by Beverly Matherne in a recent bibliographical essay *(Louisiana Studies,* March, 1972, pp. 1-12), most were intended for elementary or high school students. *The Loneliest Game,* however, a totally theatrical play designed for the professional rather than the academic theatre, marks a departure for Nolan.

The play has a long and curious history. Nolan wrote it in 1964 when his anger at the assassination of President Kennedy prompted him to ask why anyone would want to kill such a man. *The Loneliest Game* is not about the death of John Kennedy; in fact, only one allusion is made to that event. It does, however, probe the phenomenon of loneliness and suggest a reason why the lonely people—like Lee Harvey Oswald—behave as they do. It illustrates the author's belief that lonely people have a melodramatic view of the world. They see themselves as powerless and isolated victims, but at the same time, they assume that others, whom they regard as villains, are possessed of almost superhuman strength. Nolan hoped to create this melodramatic world of the lonely in the play by using the form of the melodrama for realistic dramatic purposes.

As the title suggests, the play is built around a "game" motif in which seven realistic characters are thrust into a deliberately melodramatic situation—a macabre game in which they are the pawns. The game is conducted by four melodramatic characters: Mr. Gates, his mistress Mrs. Clyme, and his two henchmen, Donne and Mute.

The realistic characters, who make up a kind of E. A. Robinson gallery of the wretched, show that the disease of loneliness is not restricted to any race, any geographical location, any sex. Nor has it anything to do with age, marital status, or degree of education. Loretta Grant is a young black schoolteacher; Billy Joe Jenkins a refugee from Mississippi; Duke Taylor a semi-literate drifter; Miss Britt an alcoholic spinster; Mr. Rogers a middle-aged librarian; Sabre Dawson a defeminized career woman, and Faye Allen a run-away housewife. They need only a

Richard Cory type to be a complete cross-section of the population.

These seven, who have only their loneliness in common, are brought to Gates' island home where they learn the terms of the game. At the end of four weeks, one of them—the one voted the loneliest by his companions—will die. The play at one level is like an Agatha Christie murder mystery. It contains familiar gothic elements—the isolated house by the sea, the sinister Vincent Price type character as the host, his equally sinister bodyguards, and the group of frightened victims who are killed off one at a time until only three are left to tell the tale.

When Nolan revised the play after seeing its try-out production, he intensified its melodramatic structure, evidently hoping to emphasize the grotesque qualities of the world the lonely create for themselves. He accomplished this by modifying the characterization of Gates, making him a creature of pure, unmotivated malignancy, and by adding the suggestion that Gates and his crew are supernatural agents of evil. This notion is foreshadowed at the end of Act I, when one of the victims refers to Gates as a devil and concludes that they are in hell. Gates' identification with Satanic forces is withheld, however, until the final scene of the play when some of the lonely who have perished in the deadly game return as assistants of Gates to help him set up the next contest. At this point, the play bears some resemblance to T. S. Eliot's *The Cocktail Party*, except that the Eliot play uses the form of the drawing room comedy into which supernatural agents for good are introduced, while *The Loneliest Game* is a melodrama with supernatural characters who are demonic.

How the lonely fall into Gates' grasp is not

clear, but the play makes the point that the lonely are susceptible to invasion by evil. Because they are weak, passive, and self-destructive, they invite evil and unwittingly cooperate with it. Actually, the lonely are never as powerless as they assume. They are, after all, a group of seven, while Gates, a cripple, and his helpers are only four. At any time, the lonely could simply overpower the deathmakers. Rogers, in fact, tries to lead the men in a revolt, but the plan fails and Miss Grant is accidentally killed.

Another possibility is that the seven could each time have voted for themselves, refusing to give Gates a victim, but after the failure of the plot, they splinter and begin using the ballot to revenge themselves upon each other. The play suggests, then, that lonely people lack the ability to act unselfishly or to bind themselves to others. Gates does not destroy them; he merely permits them to destroy themselves. They need little encouragement, for the distorted view they have of themselves and of the world makes them easy prey.

As the play ends, four of the lonely are dead: Rogers, who commits suicide after the failure of the rebellion; Loretta, who dies in the escape attempt; Jenkins, who is shot by one of Gates' men when he attempts to kill Duke Taylor; and Miss Britt—voted the loneliest. Three—Dawson, Allen, and Taylor—leave the island alive. The play suggests, however, that of the seven, only two, Miss Britt and Duke Taylor, have finally escaped the hell of loneliness.

Britt and Taylor, the two extremes in the group of victims, escape for different reasons— she because she is the most lonely and he because he is the least. Britt, moving about in her alcoholic fog, is the most withdrawn, but her role as scapegoat, her utter inability to hate, and her ultimate attainment of self-knowledge (she finally admits she is a drunkard) free her from the prison of the ego and put her beyond Gates' reach.

Taylor, on the other hand, is the most gregarious of the seven. When Gates tells his cohorts at the end of the play that he does not expect to see Duke again, he realizes that Taylor's inclusion in the group was a mistake. Superficially, he too was lonely; but his differences were radical. One trait which sets him apart, for example, is his animal instinct for survival. Duke is a man devoted to the service of self, to "looking out for number one." While this preoccupation with self makes him a less attractive character than someone like Rogers, the refined, liberal gentleman, Taylor's doggy desire to live his stringy little life becomes a positive quality in the midst of so many death wishes. Furthermore, Taylor has fewer illusions about himself than his companions. Unlike the others, who have constructed elaborate defenses, he never tries to conceal his weaknesses or pretend he is not lonely. If loneliness is an illusory hell, as the play seems to suggest, then a man with little capacity for self-deception does not belong there.

Although *The Loneliest Game* has yet to see a professional production, the play has excited a good deal of interest. The original version, called *There's Death for the Lonely* won the national Player's Workshop Award for 1963-64 and was performed by that group during the winter of 1964. After seeing his play on the stage (an experience Nolan describes in *Dramatics*, February 1967, p. 15), the playwright revised it extensively. Since that time, the play, listed in *Best Plays of 1963-64*, has been optioned to an off-Broadway producer, considered by the director of a prestigious university theatre, and finally published and favorably reviewed in *Dramatics*, May 1971, p. 10.

The play seems destined to become a favorite with academic and community theatres across the country. Its growing popularity stems no doubt from technical considerations. Directors and actors like it because while nine of the roles out of eleven are challenging and substantial, no one dominates the play. Thus, *The Loneliest Game* lends itself to ensemble playing rather than to the "star system." Moreover, it requires only one set and uses only modern costumes.

Ultimately, however, it succeeds because, in spite of the fact that it was written nearly ten years ago and inspired by a topical event, *The Loneliest Game* is a timely play. It explores in a particularly exciting way a problem which continues to plague us. Furthermore, at a time when so many plays are sloppily hammered together, this one is carefully crafted and professionally polished. At a time when interest in the nonverbal drama seems about to pall, this one is long on good dialogue. (Nolan, a student of Congreve, has never been accused, as his master was, of sacrificing plot to language, but all of his critics have commented on his acute ear.) Finally, at a time when many plays are dull and lacking in significance, *The Loneliest Game* a rattling good melodrama with a philosophical twist, has a decided appeal.

Jane F. Bonin
University of Southwestern
Louisiana, Lafayette

ACT ONE

AS THE CURTAIN RISES, MR. GATES, a large but delicately composed, middle-aged man, is examining the room with his house-keeper, MRS. CLYME. He is crippled and drags one foot. He uses a heavy cane for support, MRS. CLYME, in spite of her rather old-fashioned appearance —black dress, modest hair style—gives the impressions of being a passionate woman. Perhaps it is the deep color of her hair and eyes and the paleness of her skin. Perhaps it is that her modest dress is a bit too tight for her well-endowed body. Or perhaps it is that she moves with a cat-like sensuality. It is nothing she says. She appears to be quiet, obedient, unfeeling, impersonal, as a good servant should be.

GATES: *(Moving a chair a few feet down from the French doors awkwardly balancing himself on his cane)* Everything is in order? You are sure, Mrs. Clyme?

1

CLYME: Yes, Mr. Gates, all has been made ready.

GATES: We have everything we need? Food, drink, all that?

CLYME: Yes. All that.

GATES: Medicine?

CLYME: Yes, medicine.

GATES: Liquor?

CLYME: Everything.

GATES: Ammunition?

CLYME: I've counted everything seven times. Everything is as you ordered.

GATES: I'm not doubting you, you know. I just don't like little things to go wrong. Checked everything seven times, eh?

CLYME: Yes, sir, seven times. Seven is lucky, you know. Seven checks for seven guests. Everything will go well. I feel it.

GATES: Yes, I rather think it will. After so long a time, one gets a feeling about these things. It's almost like being an actor. One knows how the play will go as soon as the curtain goes up—even before a line is spoken. It doesn't take applause. A good actor can tell by the scent in the air. It's ... it's a feeling one gets.

CLYME: I know.

GATES: Yes, you have it, too, Mrs. Clyme, that feeling.

DONNE and MUTE have entered from the center double doors. They are dressed in black suits, white shirts, black ties; and they are carrying several suitcases. MUTE cannot speak, and neither DONNE nor MUTE ever shows emotions, although in a strange sort of way, they seem to have sympathy for each other.

GATES: *(Speaking to them, without looking at them)* They go upstairs.

DONNE: We know, Mr. Gates.

GATES: Do you have all the luggage?

DONNE: There are still a few pieces at the landing.

GATES: Don't overlook any. It disturbs my guests if they think a piece of their luggage has been misplaced. It worries them.

MUTE opens his mouth and makes a few muted gasps.

GATES: What's the matter with the mute?

DONNE: Your guests have so little that it amuses Mute to think anything could be missed.

3

GATES: When one has little, he misses much.

DONNE: Miss Dawson has four pieces.

GATES: Four is correct.

DONNE: They wanted to walk around the island.

CLYME: Like children.

DONNE: Or cats. Nobody's comfortable until he knows the lay of the land. I know the feeling.

CLYME: They shouldn't be long. We are in a small spot.

GATES: *(Turns around sharply and starts across stage, but in the middle of his speech, his cane hits against a chair, and he falls)* Each man lives in a small spot. Both the beggar and the king have to make do with six-by-six when all is said and done.

When he falls, he loses control of himself and beats the floor with his fists. MUTE sets the luggage down and leaps to help him. GATES turns in anger toward him, swinging at him with his cane.

Stay away from me, you stupid brute. I don't need any help.

MUTE cowers back, then picks up the luggage and stands fixed.

I can take care of myself. I don't need any help of animals. *(Struggles to his feet and stands a moment gaining control of himself)* Animal. Brute.

DONNE: We'll take the luggage to the rooms now.

GATES: I don't like people to touch me. I meant no offense to you, Mr. Donne.

DONNE: I was not offended, Mr. Gates.

GATES: And I meant no offense to Mute either. Tell him that.

DONNE: He can understand you. He hears.

GATES: Yes, of course, it's stupid of me. I am sorry I have offended you, Mute.

DONNE: Mute is not offended, Mr. Gates. Shall we take the luggage to the rooms now?

GATES: Yes. You know the arrangements?

DONNE: I think so. You want Mrs. Allen and Miss Dawson in the first room.

CLYME: Mrs. Allen is the wife, of course?

GATES: Of course. Her name is Faye.

CLYME: We are damnably doomed by names, aren't we? Is she ... is she beautiful?

5

GATES: I wouldn't say so. Fadingly pretty, perhaps.

CLYME: Is it necessary that she and the Dawson woman ...?

GATES: It is necessary.

CLYME: Is she to be the one?

GATES: Perhaps. I don't know yet. Not really. I never
do know at the start. Not for certain. It would take
all the meaning out of it if I know at the start. Life
would just be a cruel game, just butchery, if we
knew such things at the start. All the ritual, all
the beauty, all the sense of the scheme of things
would be gone. And there would be no need to
bring our ... our guests here. Dallas or Jackson
or Chicago, all or any would do just as well, and
with no labor to us.

CLYME: I must ask these questions.

GATES: Yes, time and again. I shall try to relieve the
monotony of the question with the elegance of the
answer. I thought I did rather well with that. *(To
DONNE)* And put the colored girl in with Miss
Britt.

DONNE: Yes, sir, that's the way you have it on the
list.

GATES: And put Taylor and Mr. Rogers in the large
room over the patio.

DONNE: There's enough space for a private room for Mr. Rogers.

GATES: Don't identify, Donne. It will only make you sorry. You are not like them anymore.

DONNE: It's not that. It's just ... he did try to commit suicide, didn't he?

GATES: That's what he pretended, at any rate. I don't have much faith in men who try to take their lives and fail. I don't trust them.

DONNE: You can't judge from that one experience ...

GATES: Don't tell me what I can or cannot judge. And don't offer suggestions. It merely distracts me. I want Mr. Rogers and Taylor in the same room. I want them together. Understand?

DONNE: All right. *(Waits, impassively)*

GATES: Well? You can go about your business now.

DONNE: What about the man from Mississippi?

GATES: Jenkins? He's on the list, isn't he?

DONNE: Yes, sir, he's on the list. But there are three unoccupied rooms.

GATES: And you have a suggestion?

DONNE: No, sir, no suggestion.

GATES: Is there an empty room next to the colored girl?

DONNE: Miss Grant? Yes, there's an empty room. It's small.

GATES: Good, put Mr. Jenkins there. And, Donne, I want Jenkins' bed right next to the colored girl's— with just a wall between them. Cheek to jowl, so to speak.

DONNE: All right, but they're thick walls.

GATES: Excellent. This is not a house of ill repute. Now, take the bags upstairs. I am growing weary.

DONNE and MUTE carry the bags upstairs.

CLYME: Is Jenkins that kind of a Southerner?

GATES: No, as a matter of fact he lost his job and was driven out of Mississippi because he offered his help in rebuilding a church that had mysteriously caught fire. Jenkins would like to be a *gentle* man, but the violence is there. He speaks softly, not from kindness, but because the violence chokes him. It will explode.

CLYME: Is he the one then?

GATES: It may be. It would be a popular choice, I think. He hasn't said more than a dozen words to the others except Mr. Rogers and Miss Grant. But, we'll just have to wait and see.

CLYME: Yes, sir.

She turns and starts upstage for the double door. GATES touches her arm, she freezes, and stops.

GATES: Have you missed me, Mrs. Clyme?

CLYME: I haven't thought of anything or anyone since I've been here. It's been peaceful, and I was tired. But I'm not anymore. I'm ready again. Perhaps it's the sea. It's always there. *(Walks to French doors)* Always there, always deep, always speaking, but never expecting an answer, never demanding. It is most restful.

GATES: And I am demanding, of course?

CLYME: Yes, you are demanding.

GATES: And you loathe me?

CLYME: *(Without passion)* Completely and fully.

GATES: And you need me?

CLYME: Yes, but not in the pauses between.

GATES: Not at all?

CLYME: Not at all.

GATES: I missed you. I would have thought you would have missed me, once or twice anyway.

CLYME: I would have.

He has moved behind her and lets his fingers play lightly on her spine.

Eventually it would have been too much, the peace, the quiet, the contentment. It would have been too much, and I would have needed you again.

GATES: Perhaps ... perhaps, I should have stayed away longer.

CLYME: *(Turns and faces him)* No. No, you stayed away long enough. Just long enough. I need you now.

They embrace passionately, then he pushes her from him.

GATES: Of course, I missed you often. But then I don't loathe you or need you, so I can enjoy the luxury.

CLYME: Yes, with you, it is a luxury.

GATES: Or, perhaps, it is different when one is out ... collecting. It's the excitement, I suppose. It ... it excites me. I missed you often.

CLYME: Are they ... are they likely to be exciting specimens?

GATES: I think so. Nothing spectacular, of course. No presidents, no movie stars, no prophets. We have to leave those for others.

CLYME: The wife, Mrs. Allen? How did you find her?

GATES: She was taking a bus to Kansas City. Or *from* Kansas City. I've forgotten which. I rode with her. It wasn't difficult.

CLYME: No, it never is.

GATES: It always comes back, doesn't it, Mrs. Clyme? But she's not like you.

CLYME: She didn't ... ? Her husband is still ... ?

GATES: Mr. Allen is, as far as I know, still in good health. The children, too. She just left. No scene. No violence.

CLYME: There are children? I wouldn't have thought so. I would think children would make a difference.

GATES: You had children.

CLYME: The best was dead. The other was like her father. You always think of girls as being like their mother. They never are, of course, unless they shouldn't be. Girls are always like the stronger. Mrs. Allen must have been very lonely.

GATES: She was almost my first choice.

CLYME: And you used her to get Miss Dawson, I suppose.

GATES: Oh, dear me, no. That would never have worked. Miss Dawson avoided her for the first few days, until the strain got too much. Our Miss Dawson thinks she's normal, you know. She lives alone, and she thinks she's normal. Oh, there may have been a friend in her boarding school days. But she has forgotten, or perhaps she just doesn't think about it anymore.

CLYME: It's all rather sad, isn't it?

GATES: Life is always sad, especially for the lonely. But we are doing what we can for them.

CLYME: Have you told them yet? Do they know why they are here?

GATES: I wouldn't even give a hint until you were present, Mrs. Clyme. I consider you more than an assistant, almost a partner.

CLYME: Thank you, Mr. Gates.

GATES: Of course, they really know; but it is our job to show them truths already known. I wonder how they shall react when I tell them.

CLYME: I hope there is no screaming. I have never liked screaming.

GATES: I think the time for screaming is past. During the first week, Mr. Rogers was close. I think he would have backed out, but he seems all right now.

CLYME: If they wanted to back out now, is it too late?

GATES: It is too late. Even if we were willing—and we have problems of our own, you know—but even if we were willing, Mrs. Clyme, our guests don't really know what they want. They couldn't stay where they were; they certainly couldn't go back to it. We are dealing with people, Mrs. Clyme, as the poet said, with "Nothing to look backward to with pride, and nothing to look forward to with hope, so now and never any different . . . ."

CLYME: I keep thinking that it might have been different.

GATES: You torment yourself to think so. And that's why you loathe me so.

CLYME: That's not the reason, Mr. Gates, not the only reason.

GATES: Sometimes you go too far, Mrs. Clyme.

CLYME: I *have* gone too far, Mr. Gates, much too far.

GATES: *(Laughs)* Of course. Sometimes I forget. With each new group, standing at the brink, sometimes I forget. You'd better see about the refreshments. They'll be coming soon.

CLYME: Yes, soon. *(Starts out)* I'll bring coffee and sandwiches. *(Turns back a moment)* You won't begin until I'm here?

GATES: It is not I who hate you, Mrs. Clyme. I gave you my word. I shall wait.

CLYME: Thank you.

She exits quickly, and GATES moves about the room, as though he were setting a stage, adjusting a chair here and there. DONNE and MUTE come down the stairs.

DONNE: Everyting is in place. We'll get the rest of the luggage now.

GATES: Can the dummy handle it alone? I wish to speak to you, Donne.

DONNE: *(Looks at MUTE)* He can handle it.

MUTE exits through the double doors. GATES waits until he has left, then he turns to DONNE.

GATES: I despise that animal.

DONNE: Yes, sir.

GATES: You don't, do you?

DONNE: Mute and I, we don't feel things the way you and Mrs. Clyme do.

GATES: Do you feel anything?

DONNE: No, nothing, or at most, merely a flutter of memory.

GATES: None of this ... excites you?

DONNE: No, none of it.

GATES: None of it? I don't understand how you go on.

DONNE: I don't go on.

GATES: I was speaking figuratively. Sometimes I think Mute speaks as much as you do.

DONNE: He does, that's true.

GATES: I will never listen to him. Never again. That brute, that senseless brute. I listened to him once. *(Turns away)* Have you made arrangements with the boat?

DONNE: It'll return in four weeks.

GATES: And their transportation back home?

DONNE: I've arranged it all. It seems like a waste of time.

GATES: We have time to waste, and it's only fair that things be ready for those who do leave. I do try to be fair about these matters. It would be easier, of course, if I didn't. Everything is more difficult for the decent man. Decency is a damnably expensive luxury. *(Slaps his crippled leg)* But I try.

DONNE: Yes, sir. You want Mute on the balcony?

GATES: Yes, it's impressive.

DONNE: And armed?

GATES: I said I want it impressive. *(Pause)* You don't have any feeling about me, do you, Donne?

DONNE: No, sir, none.

GATES: That offends me. I don't know why it should, but it does. I prefer Mrs. Clyme's hatred. Does Mute hate me?

DONNE: No, sir, he doesn't.

GATES: You know, of course?

DONNE: I know, of course.

GATES: You don't particularly like this job, do you, Donne?

DONNE: I have no feeling about it.

GATES: It doesn't even make any difference to you which one it is going to be?

DONNE: You pick them, Mr. Gates. I don't.

GATES: I don't *pick* them. *They* do the picking themselves. That's the whole point of it.

DONNE: Yes, sir.

GATES: Doesn't even make any difference if it's a man or a woman? We have three men and four women this time.

DONNE: It doesn't make any difference.

GATES: Just so much meat, is that it?

DONNE: Mute and I, we have no feelings, Mr. Gates.

MUTE enters with two suitcases.

DONNE: Take them up to the room, Mute, and then return to the balcony.

MUTE starts up the stairs.

GATES: You didn't tell him to be armed.

DONNE: He knows.

GATES: No feelings, no feelings at all. Just machines.

DONNE: Cars and bombs and high-powered rifles have no feelings, Mr. Gates.

GATES: And yet what anguish they cause.

DONNE: And clubs and kitchen knives and even little poppy seeds have no feelings.

GATES: I am reprimanded, Donne. The evil that men do is not to be blamed on the weapon. But are you only a machine, Donne?

MUTE has continued upstairs and has now disappeared. MRS. CLYME enters pushing a roll cart with sandwiches and coffee.

CLYME: No one here yet? I was sure someone would be here by this time.

GATES: You'd better bring something stronger than coffee.

CLYME: I thought they might like coffee after a walk along the seawall. The wet gets inside, you know.

GATES: I do know, but some of them will want something stronger. *(Pause)* Go ahead, Mrs. Clyme, it won't matter. They will feel sharply anyway.

CLYME: All right, I'll get the liquor. *(Exits through upstage doors)*

DONNE: She feels ... feels strongly, doesn't she?

GATES: Yes, I suppose she does. You think that odd, don't you, Donne?

DONNE: When I think about it.

GATES: But mostly you don't think, is that right?

DONNE: Could I change anything if I thought about it?

GATES: Don't even ask the question. *(Pause)* It might be well if you would stand by the doors.

DONNE moves upstage left.

Not that I think any of them will panic and try to bolt, but it can sometimes be a shock to them.

DONNE: Here, sir?

GATES: *(Moving to French doors and opening them. The sea roars)* The sea has an odd sound, hasn't it. Like it's angry or in pain. I never thought I could listen to that sound again. *(Pause)* It moves me now, strangely. It must be the loneliness in its call. Or maybe not loneliness, maybe just sympathy. I wonder what Mute hears in the sea?

DONNE: Would you like me to tell you, sir?

GATES: *(Closing the French doors and shutting out the sound of the sea)* No, don't ever tell me. I paid too much to find out, much too much.

One of the upstage doors opens and MISS BRITT, a middle-aged spinster, wearing a large hat and carrying a piece of driftwood, enters. She is followed by SABRE DAWSON, an attractive—if somewhat masculine —woman in her mid-thirties, and FAYE ALLEN, a pretty, little woman in her late twenties. MISS DAWSON and MRS. ALLEN have been holding hands and swinging them like school girls, and all three have been singing, quietly: But now all stop. MISS DAWSON and MRS. ALLEN self-consciously drop their hands, and there is a painful moment of silence.

BRITT: I found this lovely piece of driftwood. May I keep it, Mr. Gates?

GATES: Miss Britt, you may take it to your grave with you. Have you ladies been exploring our little island?

BRITT: Well, I ... that is *we (Looks at the other two with some apprehension)* ... we've been looking around. The others are still on the sea wall.

DAWSON: Is that coffee?

GATES: The housekeeper will be back in a moment. She'll pour for you. But sit down, sit down.

DAWSON: *(Going to center sofa to sit)* It's so difficult to realize that it's mid-August. In the city now, everything would be baked. Just where are we, Mr. Gates?

GATES: If you don't mind, Sabre, I would like you to sit here. *(Leads her to the sofa along the right wall)* It's every bit as comfortable, I assure you, my dear. You don't mind my calling you *Sabre*, do you, my dear?

DAWSON: *(Sitting and making an effort to cover her knees with her skirt as GATES watches her)* No, I don't mind. I don't mind at all. It's rather a foolish name I suppose.

GATES: I don't imagine many of your friends call you

Sabre, do they?

DAWSON: Well, yes, some do.

GATES: How nice. *(Turns upstage)* And, Miss Britt, would you be so good as to sit there. *(Indicates sofa upstage center)* And Mrs. Allen, if you will take the chair down there. *(Indicates the chair downstage left)* You see, my dears, *(As they take the seats he has indicated)* I am setting a stage.

BRITT: *(Laughing nervously)* That sounds a little ominous, Mr. Gates.

GATES: And you sound a little tipsy, Miss Britt. Have you been drinking?

BRITT: Why, what a thing to say. I ...

GATES: I mean no criticism, Miss Britt, just a comment.

BRITT: It sounded critical, very critical. I don't drink, Mr. Gates, except a little now and then for a cold.

GATES: It's a pity. I asked the housekeeper to bring you something.

BRITT: I ... I'm not thirsty, thank you.

GATES: I'll ask you again. Perhaps.
Mrs. Allen, you don't say much.

ALLEN: I was just thinking.

GATES: I didn't embarrass you by asking Miss Britt if she had been drinking, did I? After all, you don't like her, do you?

ALLEN: Have we done something, Mr. Gates?

DAWSON: Whatever it is, Faye and I had nothing to do with it.

GATES: My dears, you have done nothing. I told Miss Britt I meant no offense. After all, we have spent the last month together; so I assumed that after so long a friendship I should be permitted the privilege of a friend to speak the truth. Don't you agree, Miss Dawson?

DAWSON: I don't know. I've never thought about it.

GATES: Not ever having had many friends, you probably have never had to deal with the problem of privileges of friendship.

ALLEN: That's not a nice thing to say. Sabre has lots of friends.

GATES: Well, now, I seem to have offended everyone. That's the price a man pays with ladies for being crippled.

ALLEN: That has nothing to do with it.

TAYLOR and ROGERS enter from upstage

center. Both are in their late thirties or
early forties, and both appear ill at ease.
TAYLOR is dressed in a sport jacket and
wears a hat. Although his clothes are new,
on him they look second-hand. ROGERS
wears a dark summer suit.

GATES: Now, here are whole, sound men.

TAYLOR: It's a real nice place you've got here, Mr.
Gates. Kind of reminds me of an island I was on
during the war.

BRITT: Were you in the war, Mr. Taylor?

TAYLOR: I told you about that, Miss Britt. *(Starts to
sit down next to her)*

GATES: When he told you, he had his hat off. That's
the reason you don't remember.

TAYLOR: Oh, damn it, I forgot. *(Removes hat)*

BRITT: I guess it's hard for an oil man like you to remember about hats. I don't suppose you wear hats
much in your oil field, do you, Mr. Taylor?

TAYLOR: That's the truth, ma'am, except the tin kind,
of course.

GATES: Duke, why don't you sit down over there and
keep Miss Dawson company. She likes strong,
outdoor men, whole men.

23

TAYLOR: Well sure, if Miss Dawson don't mind.

GATES: Why should she mind? It's my davenport.

MISS DAWSON moves down to the downstage end of the sofa, and TAYLOR sits down nervously on the upstage end. GATES turns upstage to ROGERS who has stood watching.

GATES: Mr. Rogers, won't you take that chair there? *(Indicates a chair upstage left in front of the French windows)*

ROGERS: *(Going to chair and sitting)* It's almost as though you were setting a stage, Mr. Gates.

GATES: That's most observant, Mr. Rogers. That's exactly what I am doing. *(To DONNE)* Donne, would you go out and tell the last two to come in.

DONNE: Yes, sir.

He starts out as MRS. CLYME enters with a second roll cart, this with various bottles of liquor, an ice bucket, and some glasses. He waits until she enters, then exits, closing the door behind him. MUTE appears on the balcony and stands there. ROGERS looks up at MUTE for a long moment. TAYLOR looks at ROGERS, then he too looks at MUTE.

GATES: Yes, the stage is almost set. Soon we'll be ready.

CLYME: *(Stopping the liquor cart upstage left)*
Yes, almost ready. The reason will soon be clear.

DAWSON: Reason for what? This is all ... all very odd.

GATES: Would you like some coffee, Miss Dawson?

DAWSON: *(Rising)* No, I don't think so. I think I'll ...
well, to be honest ... I'm beginning to have a
headache. It's nothing serious, but I think I'll just
go to my room and rest a bit. If you'll all excuse
me. *(Starts to leave)*

GATES: Miss Dawson, are you ill?

DAWSON: No. No, it's really nothing.

GATES: Good. Then please sit down.

DAWSON: *(Sitting)* Well ... I guess ... I mean ...

ALLEN: *(Attempting to defend MISS DAWSON)*
You must be planning something very important to
make a person stay here when she's sick.

GATES: It's most important, Mrs. Allen. It's as important as catching a bus. And you know, Mrs.
Allen, how important that can be. *(Pause)* Don't
you, Mrs. Allen?

*MRS. ALLEN draws into herself, and
GATES turns upstage to MRS. CLYME.*

Where the devil are the other two?

CLYME: They are coming. Maybe I could serve the coffee.

GATES: All right, serve the damned coffee. Miss Britt, would you be so good as to help her?

BRITT: *(Rising)* I don't think I really want any coffee.

TAYLOR: I don't either.

GATES: *(Ignoring them both)* Miss Dawson will have coffee, Mrs. Clyme. Black, I believe. You do take your coffee black, don't you, Miss Dawson? *(Pauses)* Did you hear me, Miss Dawson?

DAWSON: I heard you, yes.

GATES: Why does everyone act in slow motion. You are not dead yet.

ROGERS: An impending catastrophe always appears to be happening in slow motion, Mr. Gates.

GATES: Thank you, Mr. Rogers, thank you. Is that the way it seemed to you when you jumped from that bridge?

ROGERS: Is that intended to shock me into silence, Mr. Gates? All right, I'll be silent.

GATES: Miss Dawson, how do you want your coffee?

DAWSON: Black. Black, black, black, black.

LORETTA GRANT, a light-colored Negro, youngish, tall, and thin and wearing glasses enters. She is followed by BILLY JOE JEN-KINS, who in spite of city dress, yet looks rural. They are obviously embarrassed, but they seem at ease with each other—the way shy people sometimes are when they have walked together alone and forgotten them-selves. They have entered the room after Gates' question: so they have heard Miss Dawson's outburst without knowing the cause. The outburst—and the word—has made them painfully aware of the world of "other people," people who say things that hurt for reasons they never really under-stand, or want to understand.

GATES: Did you two have a nice walk?

JENKINS: Very nice. I guess we're late. We got to talk-ing.

GATES: You have kept us all waiting, but we under-stand. We know how you Southerners are when you get to talking. You forget time completely.

GRANT: I'm not from the South, Mr. Gates. My home is New Jersey. I was born there.

JENKINS: I worked one summer at a plant right near Riverside, that's her home. That's what we were talking about.

GATES: A most remarkable coincidence. I thought per-haps you had discovered mutual relatives.

27

GRANT: No, Mr. Gates, no mutual relatives, except Adam, of course.

JENKINS: Or, maybe Noah.

GATES: *(Annoyed at their recovery)* Miss Grant, would you be so good as to sit over there with Miss Dawson and Mr. Taylor? Miss Dawson lived in New Jersey for a time. Perhaps you were neighbors.

GRANT: If you like.

She starts across the room. GATES watches her; and then just as she reaches his position in the room, he turns quickly away from her to start downstage. She accidentally bumps his cane, knocking him off balance. He half falls to the floor. She moves quickly to help him.

GATES: *(Obviously in pain as he breaks his fall)* Get back and leave me alone. *(Struggles to his feet)* Don't ever touch me.

She stands almost paralyzed by his anger and agony.

I'm sorry, Miss Grant. I don't like to be touched. By anyone.

GRANT: I understand, Mr. Gates.

She walks to sofa and sits. Both MISS DAW-

SON and TAYLOR move just slightly away from her, almost involuntarily.

GATES: Do you, Miss Grant? It's not that I mind you personally.

GRANT: I know. When one is ... handicapped ... he needs to do things for himself.

GATES: That's most interesting. *(Pauses)* Do you need those glasses, Miss Grant?

GRANT: *(Laughs)* I'd be almost blind without them.

GATES: That's interesting. May I see them?

She hands him the glasses, and he holds them up.

They are strong.

GRANT: Did I say *almost* blind? Everything is just a kind of fuzzy whiteness to me.

GATES: That is too bad. *(Drops the glasses on the floor)* How clumsy of me. *(Stamps his crippled leg on the glasses)* And now I've broken them.

JENKINS: *(Starting forward)* That was a rotten thing to do, and you did it on purpose.

GATES: *(Without looking at him)* Sit down, Mr. Jenkins. Sit down, I said.

29

JENKINS: If you think just because you've given us a vacation, you can bully us around, you ...

GATES: Sit down, Jenkins.

MUTE steps out of view for a moment and returns with a rifle across his arm.

JENKINS: The hell I'm going to sit down.

GATES: Look up on the balcony, Mr. Jenkins. It will be hell if you don't.

JENKINS looks around the room. All the others look down at their hands.

JENKINS: Isn't anyone else going to say anything?

GRANT: It's all right, Billy Joe. You'd better do what he says.

GATES: Sit down, Mr. Jenkins. Up there.

JENKINS sits on upstage center sofa. He looks about for a moment, trying to establish his courage, and then sinks down.

Miss Britt will join you there in a moment as soon as she is finished helping Mrs. Clyme. Perhaps you could entertain her with your Rebel yells. Now, we were just serving some refreshments. Miss Dawson, you wanted coffee. Black. Mrs. Clyme, will you please give Miss Dawson her coffee. She has been most patient.

30

MRS. CLYME brings coffee to MISS DAW-SON as GATES continues.

And, Miss Grant, what would you like? We have gin. *(Pauses)* Now, Miss Grant, you aren't going to let a little thing like a pair of glasses ruin this lovely vacation, are you? After all, you were the one who said that handicapped people need to do things for themselves.

GRANT: I had my glasses, Mr. Gates, just as you have your cane.

GATES: Oh, is that all. *(Turns to DONNE)* Donne, bring Miss Grant one of my extra canes. *(Back to GRANT)* Now, that should make everything all right.

MISS GRANT withdraws. DONNE steps outside for a moment, returns with a cane and places it on Miss Grant's lap. All the while, GATES continues.

GATES: So, now would you like some gin? I asked you, Miss Grant, if you would like some gin? No. Well, it's here if you want it. And, Mr. Taylor, would you like something?

TAYLOR: *(Clearing his throat)* Well, maybe a little whiskey.

GATES: Not oil? I thought Texas oil millionaires drank nothing but oil. All of you know that Mr. Taylor here is a Texas oil millionaire, don't you?

TAYLOR: I only said that because you asked me to, Mr. Gates.

GATES: Of course, and I'm grateful, Duke. But you did enjoy playing the part, didn't you?

TAYLOR: I guess so. Sure, I liked it. It was nice once in my life to feel that nobody could push me around. Even if it was all a lie.

GATES: That's a good answer, Duke. A good manly answer. I wish you were an oil millionaire. Miss Britt, would you bring Duke a glass of whiskey for his manly answer?

MISS BRITT pours whiskey into a glass, and starts to put ice in it.

TAYLOR: If that's for me, Miss Britt, you can leave out the ice.

MISS BRITT carries the glass of warm whiskey to him as GATES continues.

GATES: Mr. Jenkins, we don't have mint juleps or Mississippi moonshine, but we have everything else.

JENKINS: I don't want anything.

GATES: A pity. Mr. Rogers?

ROGERS: Nothing.

GATES: Mrs. Allen?

ALLEN: I'll ... I'll have a little bourbon and some ice, please. If you have it.

GATES: Of course. Mrs. Clyme, would you be so good as to take care of Mrs. Allen.

> *CLYME fixes the drink and MISS BRITT stands watching her, licking her upper lip.*

And, Miss Britt, since you're already there, perhaps you might fix your own drink. That is, if you are drinking.

> *MISS BRITT pours whiskey over ice in a glass as CLYME carries the glass to MRS. ALLEN. Then MISS BRITT takes the glass and returns to her seat next to JENKINS. During this action, GATES surveys the scene with satisfaction, and the others occupy themselves by looking nervously at their hands.*

Now, things are really shaping up. We are all on stage now—the whole cast. And now our little comic opera is ready to begin.

ROGERS: And you're ready to give us the plot?

GATES: I like that, Mr. Rogers. You picked up my metaphor nicely. It's such a pleasure to converse with an educated man. I am almost ready to forgive you for jumping from that bridge.

ROGERS: I didn't know that my affairs had offended you, Mr. Gates. The police perhaps, but why you?

GATES: Didn't I tell you, Mr. Rogers? This leg—this lovely twisted thing—I wasn't born with it. It was a gift, a gift from a crazy suicide who pulled me over with him when I tried to stop him from jumping. You see, Mr. Rogers, I have been offended.

ROGERS: Not by me.

GRANT: Nor me. I never even saw you before you came to me.

ALLEN: I never even heard of you. No one here ever did.

GATES: No one? That dummy did. Mute there was the man I tried to save. *(Pause)* But that's neither here nor there. You are not here because you have offended me. You are here to be helped, and we are here to keep you from offending society.

DAWSON: I don't need any help.

BRITT: I've never hurt anyone in my whole life.

JENKINS: If you want to help society, do something about the brutes—the people who bomb churches and break other people's hearts and glasses.

GATES: Oh, society can handle them. There's the

34

F.B.I. and the Attorney General's office, and the K.K.K. and all sorts of organizations to save us from the openly dangerous. But it's not the openly dangerous we have to fear. It's the lonely, frustrated, little people who would never hurt anyone intentionally and then out of that same lovely loneliness kill the best things they can find.

ROGERS: And this all has something to do with your comic opera plot, I assume?

GATES: Ah, Mr. Rogers, you do like to pursue your metaphor. Yes, it has a great deal to do with my plot—but perhaps it won't be quite so comic opera.

ROGERS: Oh, you plan a tragedy?

GATES: A melodrama, Mr. Rogers. One of you is going to die.

BRITT: All of us are going to die. *(Rising)* May I fix myself another drink? *(Goes to liquor cart)*

GATES: True, Miss Britt, true. You and the bottle have found wisdom. But only one of you will be executed here four weeks from today. The rest of you can take care of your dying as best as you can.

TAYLOR: Damn it, I knew it. I knew as soon as somebody offered to do something decent for me, there would be a catch. Ah, the hell with it. Is it okay if I get another drink, too?

GATES: No, it is not all right. Don't you people understand what I'm saying? Four weeks from today, one of you will be taken out and shot.

GRANT: Would you like me to ask why?

GATES: You're all so damned smug in your despair. You think you have nothing to worry about. You've all tried to die—at least once—and so you think that it won't make any difference to you if you're killed. Well, you're wrong. You'll care. You'll sweat. You'll live ten thousand years that last morning. Ask Mute up there. He could tell you what it's like to watch yourself dying. He can tell you, and he can't even talk.

GRANT: I'm not smug, Mr. Gates, and I'm not in despair. I don't want to die, and I never tried to kill myself. I don't know what you've heard, and you've wrong about me.

TAYLOR: I never tried to bump myself off neither.

JENKINS: Nor did I.

DAWSON: Well, I never did either. I never even thought about it.

GATES: Oh, didn't you? You're all perfectly normal people, aren't you? Why do you think I've gathered you all together? Do you know what it is that you all have in common? You ought to be able to recognize the disease in each other. You don't even belong on earth, don't you know that? You were born someplace and left it to go someplace that doesn't exist. Take Jenkins there. He'll tell you that he had to leave Mississippi because he helped build a church some of his worthy neighbors had bombed.

JENKINS: I wouldn't tell *you* anything, Mr. Gates.

GATES: The truth is that he helped build the church so he could leave. If he had had to bomb the church instead, he'd have done that—just as easily. He left something he didn't want to go someplace he wasn't wanted—or at least he didn't think he was, and that's even worse. Or what about Duke there? He never left any place. He never was any place. He's a drifter.

TAYLOR: I was in the army four years. That's someplace.

GATES: Yes, four years. Four years cleaning out mess halls and latrines.

TAYLOR: I saw action. I got it in my service record. I was at Manila.

GATES: Yes, cleaning out mess halls and latrines.

TAYLOR: It don't make no difference. I got a battle ribbon.

GATES: I'm not trying to humiliate you, Duke. I wish you were somebody, something, even a Texas oil millionaire. But you're not. Have you ever been to Texas, Duke?

TAYLOR: Sure, lots of times. Houston, Fort Worth...

GATES: And Dallas, of course. Digging potatoes, washing cars, sweeping up warehouses.

ROGERS: Is this some sort of a psychological experiment? Just what do you expect of us?

GATES: Little, Mr. Rogers. Little. You have the freedom of this little island for four weeks, and then all of you except the one to be executed will be returned to his—I almost said *home*—but you'll be returned to your desired destination, no worse off for the experience. In fact, you'll be better off. You'll have rid the world of a potential menace. The ritual—if you survive it—will help cleanse your souls.

ROGERS: And have you selected the sacrificial goat for this little ritual of yours?

GATES: Oh, no, you are to do that. Each week, we will vote, and in four weeks, the one winning the election will be executed. It's really very simple.

DAWSON: You're insane. Utterly insane. Who are you? Who are you really?

GATES: Well, I'm not Faye's husband; so this is not an act of revenge. I like to think of myself as the Voice of Decent Humanity, crying out against the centuries of havoc let loose by the lonely people. I'm the million men who died because of a house painter in Austria; I'm the millions who grieved because of a psychopath in Dallas. I'm ...

ALLEN: You are insane. You really are.

GATES: It doesn't matter who *I* am. It matters who *you* are. You're a collection of lonely derelicts, and one of you is going to be executed to purge the rest of us.

GRANT: I never considered myself a lonely derelict. I teach school and I don't hurt anyone.

GATES: You're lonely. I'm not saying it's your fault, but when one has the plague, it doesn't make any difference whose fault it is.

JENKINS: All right, we're lonely. But is that some kind of a crime?

GATES: It leads to crime—little crimes like shooting a king, big crimes like war.

BRITT: *(Who has been standing at the liquor table, sipping and pouring drinks, now returns to her seat)* I'm not lonely. I'm not lonely at all.

GATES: You will be when you sober up, and then some young intern who has better things to do will have to race through the streets to pump sleeping pills out of your stomach.

ROGERS: We've all been tried and found guilty, is that it?

GATES: In a word, yes.

ROGERS: Then why this whole business? Why don't you just kill us and be done with it?

GATES: Extermination never works. It only fattens the beast. Hilter exterminated ten million people and there are ten times ten million to take their place. The Inquisition reached the souls by selective execution, and centuries from now, the wounds will still bleed. I want one sacrifice, one—that's all. Four weeks from now, if that one has been selected in common agreement, you'll have been purged.

ALLEN: I couldn't vote for someone else to die.

GATES: Of course not, my dear. I wouldn't ask that of you. You simply vote for the person who is most lonely. Anyone. Miss Grant because she belongs to a lonely, sad race? Miss Britt because she can't breathe out of a bottle? Mr. Taylor because everyone hates him on sight? Just anyone.

TAYLOR: I knew you'd get to me.

ROGERS: If you just want a victim, I'll volunteer. You don't have to wait four weeks. You can kill me now.

GATES: I don't want a volunteer, and if I did, Mr. Rogers, you wouldn't be any good. You wouldn't last four weeks. You'd botch it. Well, that's your problem, to find the most lonely among yourselves. We'll have an election once a week. On the last election, four weeks from now, one of you will stay and die and the rest will be free to go. Now, are there any questions?

JENKINS: I have one. Why don't you go to hell?

GATES: I would tell you, Mr. Jenkins, but you wouldn't understand. Yet.

He starts upstage for the door.

TAYLOR: *(Muttering to himself)* He's right. Everybody does hate me on sight.

GATES: *(Turning back)* Oh, I almost forgot. There are some sandwiches there if any of you are hungry.

TAYLOR: *(Rising)* Well, why the hell not? *(Crosses over to tray of sandwiches, takes a fistful, and jams one in his mouth)* I might as well eat as much as I can.

GATES: You are, of course, my guests; and anything you want, I'll supply. But don't try to leave the island. It's thirty miles to shore, and I believe there are sharks.

GATES exits through upstage door, followed by MRS. CLYME and DONNE. MUTE disappears up the stairs.

ALLEN: It's a kind of dream, isn't it. This can't be

real. It's a joke maybe.

BRITT: It's rather like an Agatha Christie mystery. Except, of course, we know the murderer. We just don't know the victim.

TAYLOR: Look, let's do this fair. Let's draw lots or play a game of poker or something. That's the only fair way to pick someone.

JENKINS: *(Rising)* Hell, you're not all going to take him seriously, are you?

ROGERS: It's mad, but it's real, and he's serious. But we're not going to draw lots. *(Rises)* All my life, I've seen the way things are, and I've let them carry me along. All right, we're lonely people. We're used to being pushed around by somebody else, maybe even used to dying when somebody yells drop dead. But this is one chance for us to be different. We're not going to give him his victim. We're not going to say, "All right, take Czecho-slovakia." We're going to fight him.

JENKINS: You can count on me. I'd like to punch that fat face of his right off his shoulders.

ALLEN: *(Rising)* The main thing is that we have got to stick together.

GRANT: *(Rising and holding the cane in both hands)* I've never hated anyone in my whole life, but I could kill that man.

DAWSON: *(Rising)* He's a devil, a real devil.

TAYLOR: *(Rising)* We'll stick together.

ROGERS: There are seven of us, and together—together—we'll stop him.

BRITT: *(Still sitting and holding her drink)* We won't stop him. We won't stop him at all.

DAWSON: If you'll stop drinking, we'll stop him.

ROGERS: Why can't we stop him? He's only a man—and a crippled man at that. If we all stay together, why can't we stop him?

BRITT: *(Far off)* Miss Dawson said it. Mr. Gates is *the* devil, and we're all in hell. *(Sips her drink slowly)* It's not as bad as I had feared.

CURTAIN

ACT TWO

The same scene, two weeks later. It is Sunday evening. The French doors are open wide; the sea is loud, but monotonous, and a slight wind blows the folds of the drapes at the edges of the French doors. The lights are on in the room, but except for the downstage left area, they appear dim. As the curtain rises, ROGERS is sitting on a chair, downstage left, playing a game of chess on a small table in front of him. He moves a piece, studies the play for a moment and then puts it back. He makes a second move, keeping his hand on the piece, then returns it. He then sits back and studies the board. TAYLOR enters from center upstage doors, walks down, and watches him as he again moves pieces and returns them to their original position.

TAYLOR: Still playing chess by yourself, eh?

ROGERS: Yes.

TAYLOR: You haven't got very far.

ROGERS: No, I haven't.   *(Moves a piece and then returns it)*

TAYLOR: You'll never get through that game, if you don't follow through on your moves.

ROGERS: I can't figure a line of attack.

TAYLOR: Do you want to play me a game?

ROGERS: No, no thank you.

TAYLOR: I'm pretty good.

ROGERS: I'm sure you are.

TAYLOR: I played a lot when I was in service. A guy I knew in service taught me.

ROGERS: Good.

TAYLOR: Of course, I don't know any of them book plays, but I don't think that means much, do you?

ROGERS: No.

TAYLOR: It takes all the fun out of the game. Don't you think so?

ROGERS: I guess so.

TAYLOR: You'd still rather play by yourself, right?

ROGERS: Right.

TAYLOR: Probably rather room alone, too, wouldn't you?

ROGERS: No, it doesn't make any difference.

TAYLOR: There's something wrong with me, isn't there?

ROGERS: Probably with me.

TAYLOR: *(Walks to the other side of the room)* No, it's me. Gates is right; everybody hates me on sight. Even when I was in the Army, it was the same thing. Nobody wanted to bunk around me. Even in the damned Army. *(Pause)* You know something. I wanted to stay in. But they didn't want me. Even the damned Army didn't want me.

ROGERS: Probably just your imagination.

TAYLOR: Imagination hell. The damned lieutenant told me. Kept me in the whole damned war and then threw me out. *(Sits down on the sofa)* Said I wasn't well enough educated. Couldn't pass their damned tests. You know I couldn't read my own name when I went in the service.

ROGERS: You could have learned.

TAYLOR: Wouldn't have done any good. I did learn some. I was on this here island, a place called Canton. Sure was a lonely place. And there was this sergeant, he taught me how to read and write. Pretty good, I thought. The captain wanted to give me a promotion, but I had to read and write first. Just to make PFC. I spent a whole year working on it. A whole year. Got so I was pretty good. *(Jumps up, goes to bookcase, and grabs a book)* Look, I'll show you I can read. *(Opens book)* Hell, it's poetry.

ROGERS: That's all right, Taylor, I believe you.

TAYLOR: No, I want to show you ... even with poetry. Listen *(Starts reading haltingly)* "Mr. Flood's Party by E. A. Robinson. Old Eben Flood, climbing alone one night *(Pause)* Over the hill between the town below *(Pause)* And the forsaken *(Pause)* hermitage *(Pause)* That held as much as he should ever know *(Pause)* On earth again of home, paused warily." *(Bungles* warily) Hell, I can't make sense of that.

ROGERS: *(Half to himself)* "The road was his with not a native near; And Eben having leisure, said aloud, For no man else in Tilbury Town to hear: 'Well, Mr. Flood, we have the harvest moon Again ...."

TAYLOR: You know it by heart?

ROGERS: Yes, I know it by heart.

TAYLOR: Is it pretty good?

ROGERS: It's all right.

TAYLOR: *(Putting book back)* What's it about?

ROGERS: It's about a drunk.

TAYLOR: Like Miss Britt, eh?

ROGERS: Yes, very much like Miss Britt. "A Valiant armor of scarred hopes outworn."

TAYLOR: Oh. Well, I guess I'll never understand that

stuff. But I'm not stupid.

ROGERS: I'm sure you're not.

TAYLOR: I'm a good chess player. That takes brains, doesn't it?

ROGERS: *(Pushing the chess pieces together on the board)* A great deal more than I have.

TAYLOR: *(Going back to sofa)* Life's something like a game of chess, isn't it?

ROGERS: Some people have said so.

TAYLOR: Like take us. The seven of us, we're pawns. Gates, he's the king. Mrs. Clyme, she's the queen; and those two characters—Mute and Donne—they're knights.

ROGERS: And that doesn't give us much chance to win, does it?

TAYLOR: None at all. Anytime the pawns even get close to the queen or knights, the power can just reach out and grab them. I figured this all out. We don't stand a chance. So you know what I'm going to do? I'm just going to enjoy myself. The food's good, the liquor's good; and if I end up dead, I end up dead.

ROGERS: Seven pawns, a king, a queen, two knights. It isn't much of a match. *(Moves all the players off the board, except for seven pawns on one side and the King, Queen, and two Knights on the other)* It even looks stupid. Poor old pawns. They can just hobble around until they're picked off. One block at a time. *(He moves the pawns on the board)*

TAYLOR: Miss Britt might even be right. Gates may be the devil. He certainly acts like one.

ROGERS: *(Looking at the board)* There might be one chance of winning, just one. If the pawns could attack the King, they might force a stalemate.

TAYLOR: Not much chance of that. The other powers would pick them off.

ROGERS: *(Rising)* I've been thinking in terms of getting Mute and Donne, but they move too fast. They're ready for an attack. But the King. *(Lifts the King piece and looks at it and then sets it back on the board)* But the King, he's not ready for anything. *(Goes to TAYLOR)* If we can get Gates, we can get control here.

TAYLOR: Yeah, we can get killed trying.

ROGERS: All of them hate him—Mrs. Clyme, Mute, Donne. You can see it. If we got control, they would do what we said. And if we can get Gates, we've got control.

TAYLOR: Well, maybe, but I still say all we'll do is get killed trying.

ROGERS: Don't you want to get out of this place?

TAYLOR: Yeah, sure, yeah, I guess so. I don't mind it here though. I've been in a lot worse places. The food's good and I don't have to do anything.

ROGERS: Damn it. Do you want to die here?

TAYLOR: Well, no, I don't want to die here. But I don't think that's really going to happen.

ROGERS: You think it's all a joke? Well, it's not. Gates means what he says. One of us is going to die.

TAYLOR: Well, maybe he does. Maybe he does.

ROGERS: There's no maybe about it.

TAYLOR: All right then, let's say one of us is going to die. I don't think it's going to be me. I mean I don't think that I am going to get the votes. The way that Dawson dame and Mrs. Allen have been .... Well, that's bad enough with men, but women. God, it's disgusting.

ROGERS: What are you suggesting? That finally in moral indignation, we'll vote for one of them?

TAYLOR: No, I didn't mean that exactly. Hell, look, I've done everything you suggested. The first time I voted for myself just like you said. And in the voting today, I voted for Gates. That was a good idea. I'll bet that shook him.

ROGERS: We've got to do more than shake him.

TAYLOR: But when it finally comes down to it, when we finally have to vote, I think it will be someone else. That colored girl, for instance.

ROGERS: What?

TAYLOR: Well, I mean ... hell, after all *we* ought to stick together.

ROGERS: Taylor, you get one thing straight. If it ever does come to that kind of a vote, you'll get mine. Yes, and I'll be damned glad to give it to you, too.

TAYLOR: Now, you're mad at me. You just don't like me, do you?

ROGERS: *(Turns away)* I'm sorry I said that. You can't help the way you think, I suppose.

TAYLOR: I ain't saying I mean any harm to anybody. I'm just saying that if ... well, I just don't think it will be me. Don't tell me you haven't thought of that, too. It wouldn't be you.

ROGERS: If anyone dies, it will be me, too. *(Turns away and speaks almost to himself)* I couldn't stand it again—just standing there and being frightened while someone else died.

TAYLOR: What's that?

ROGERS: *(Turning back)* Do you think even if you got

away, you could ever live with yourself again, to think about that ... that obscenity, Gates, just playing with us like damned chess pieces, like pawns.

TAYLOR: I ain't never been anything else. I don't like it, but I can live with it. If people will just let me, I can live fine. I ain't like the rest of you. I never expected to be anything else but lonely, and it doesn't bother me anymore.

ROGERS: You've got to try.

TAYLOR: Oh, hell, sure, I'll try. If it ain't too risky.

ROGERS: If I figure out a plan, will you go along with it?

TAYLOR: Why sure, Mr. Rogers, I'll do anything you say. Well, almost anything. If there's any kind of a chance, I'm willing to try it.

ROGERS: All right, I've got a plan. It takes just three of us.

TAYLOR: Three?

ROGERS: We'll need Jenkins.

TAYLOR: I ain't sure I trust him. He's out walking with that colored girl again. And him a Southerner, too. He'd rather be with her than his own kind.

ROGERS: Would you go and get him?

TAYLOR: If it's just a woman he wants, I think Mrs. Allen sort of goes for him. *(Snickers)* At least, that Dawson dame looks at the two of them as though she's afraid they will get something going. People sure are funny.

ROGERS: Will you go get him, please?

TAYLOR: I'll look for him. Do you want the colored girl, too?

ROGERS: No. There's no sense in getting the women into it unless we have to.

TAYLOR: Couldn't get them all in anyway. Miss Britt is passed out most of the time. She wouldn't even vote in the election.

ROGERS: If you should see Miss Dawson and Mrs. Allen .... .

TAYLOR: They were sitting on the sea wall a little while ago.

ROGERS: If you should see them, don't say anything to them.

TAYLOR: Wouldn't do any good if you did. It's a funny thing. They were very polite to me when they thought I was an oil millionaire, but now they don't hardly see me.

ROGERS: Would you please go now?

TAYLOR: Sure, I'll go. Right now. *(Starts toward up-stage door)* If this plan is too risky, I'm not in. I mean .... Hell, I'll go get Jenkins.

He exits and ROGERS returns to the chess table. He lines the seven pawns up opposite the king, queen, and two knights. He looks up at the balcony, lifts a knight piece and sets it on a side block. He lifts the queen, looks at it, and sets it off the board, but near the edge. He rises and looks around the room, then goes to the French doors and looks out. He stands for a moment as if in a trance; the stage lights dim a little, and the roar of the sea increases in volume. He starts toward the patio, stops abruptly, closes the French doors and stands with his back to them. From the hall beyond the up-stage center doors comes a tapping sound, Gates' cane hitting upon the bare floor. ROGERS listens nervously, watching the up-stage doors. One door opens: the stage lights go up slowly, and GATES enters, followed by DONNE. ROGERS immediately looks to-ward the balcony; and MUTE, with a rifle in his hands, appears. DONNE looks about the room, signals MUTE, and MUTE disappears up the stairs. GATES looks at ROGERS and then walks to the chess table. DONNE takes a position upstage left.

GATES: Have you given up on your chess for the evening, Mr. Rogers?

ROGERS: Yes.

GATES: I don't play chess myself. It seems such a sil-

54

ly game.

ROGERS: It is, if you only like to play when you have all the power.

GATES: Oh, I see. I am the King here... *(Nudges the King piece)* Mrs. Clyme is, I guess, the Queen over here; and Donne and Mute are the Knights. All of you are the opposing pawns, I would guess.

ROGERS: I thought you didn't play chess.

GATES: I don't ... anymore. *(Pause)* You're not trying to figure out your problem on a chess table, are you, Mr. Rogers?

ROGERS: Certainly not. I ... wasn't even playing a game. I was just toying with the pieces.

GATES: You don't like to tell the truth, do you, Mr. Rogers?

ROGERS: Not particularly.

GATES: Not even to yourself. So it wouldn't do me any good to ask you why you are standing there with your back to the sea?

ROGERS: I had just closed the doors.

GATES: Oh?

ROGERS: *(Moving into center stage)* I was cold.

GATES: Oh? I thought it might have been the roar of the sea.

ROGERS: No.

GATES: I thought perhaps you heard the sea calling you to come and end it all.

ROGERS: Is that what it calls to you?

GATES: *(Laughs)* Mr. Rogers, I'm afraid you have mistaken our little game. I am not the great hunter looking for the most dangerous game. I should certainly have selected more dangerous beasts for such a game.

ROGERS: Oh, I thought we were dangerous.

GATES: Like bubonic-carrying rats, Mr. Rogers, not like tigers. That's an unfortunate comparison, I know. And I do not mean to offend you. I like you, Mr. Rogers, and I am trying to be your friend.

ROGERS: Well, friend, then just let me say that I am not planning to jump into the sea—no matter what the waves say to you.

GATES: I'm pleased you are no longer tempted. Already our little experiment is making you stronger. *(Pause)* Incidentally, you can change rooms if Taylor annoys you.

ROGERS: He doesn't.

GATES: I'm pleased. When one brings people together, he takes such a responsibility. I am often quite distressed by the results.

ROGERS: I'm sure you are.

GATES: Not for Miss Dawson and Mrs. Allen, of course. They would have found each other anyway. But look at Miss Grant and Jenkins. Who would have thought that a Mississippian and a Negro school teacher would become such ... such good friends.

ROGERS: I am not surprised, but I am sure you are. We are people with problems, Mr. Gates, but we are people—not just problems. We have feelings other than loneliness, and thoughts for other things besides ourselves. We have our weaknesses, but we, also, have our strengths.

GATES: Oh, do you?

ROGERS: We do.

GATES: *(Turns away)* Did you know that Miss Grant won today's balloting?

ROGERS: You rather like lying too, don't you, Mr. Gates?

GATES: It's true I got five votes, and there was one blank—Miss Britt, I assume. But then I am not a candidate. And Miss Grant got one vote.
(Turns back to ROGERS)

ROGERS: I don't think you'll be satisfied with one vote.

GATES: There'll be more. Miss Grant didn't vote for herself. I wonder who did. Jenkins, maybe? Southerners have always loved the Negro, but it hasn't kept them from killing them. I guess that's too complex for Jenkins. Maybe Taylor. Or maybe Mrs. Allen. I think she's about ready to trade Miss Dawson for Jenkins. I don't suppose it was you, Mr. Rogers?

ROGERS returns to chess table and fixes his eyes on the pieces.

I don't really think so, but you know something odd, Mr. Rogers, you do look guilty.

GATES turns and goes upstage through the center doors, DONNE follows him. MISS BRITT, looking sick, comes down the stairs.

BRITT: All alone, Mr. Rogers? I thought I heard voices.

ROGERS: It was Gates. He's left. *(Pause)* How are you feeling, Miss Britt?

BRITT: Not very well. I wanted to see Mr. Gates. I think there is something wrong with the water. I was very sick this afternoon, and I'm sure it's the water. I have a rather delicate constitution.

She sits on the upstage sofa. ROGERS continues playing with the chess pieces.

I wonder where everyone is?

ROGERS: Out walking.

BRITT: Don't you like walking, Mr. Rogers?

ROGERS: Sometimes.

BRITT: *(Rising)* Well, I think I'll take a walk. Perhaps I may find some more driftwood. *(Starts toward door)* You wouldn't like to walk with me, would you, Mr. Rogers?

ROGERS: No. No, thank you.

BRITT: Then I guess I shall have to walk alone. *(Starts out)*

ROGERS: *(Rising)* Miss Britt?

BRITT: Yes?

ROGERS: Did you see anyone when you came down from your room just now?

BRITT: No, no one. Except that man with the gun.

ROGERS: Mute?

BRITT: I think that's what Mr. Gates calls him.

ROGERS: What was he doing?

BRITT: He was just sitting there, not reading or anything. I spoke to him, but he didn't even see me.

ROGERS: Oh. *(Turns back downstage)* Thank you, Miss Britt, thank you.

BRITT: You're sure you don't want to go for a walk?

ROGERS: What?

BRITT: Would you like to take a walk?

ROGERS: Oh, no thank you, no thank you.

BRITT: Well, then, I'll see you shortly.

> *BRITT exits through upstage doors. ROGERS turns upstage and looks about room. He looks up at the balcony, moving under it so that he can see beyond the turn. Then he stands with his back against the wall to estimate if he could be seen from the balcony. He moves a chair from near the French doors and props it under the handle of the upstage doors and tries the doors to see if they can be opened. Satisfied that the chair will hold, he steps back to view the scene again. Then he turns the lights off with a switch on the upstage wall, leaving the stage in darkness. There is a fumbling at the door. Then voices outside.*

TAYLOR: *(Outside)* Hey, what's wrong with this door?

ROGERS: *(Turns on the lights)* Just a minute.

He removes the chair, opens the door, and JENKINS and TAYLOR enter, and ROGERS closes the door behind them.

TAYLOR: What was wrong with the door?

ROGERS: Nothing.

He draws the two men downstage towards the French doors.

I think I have an idea.

TAYLOR: Nothing risky. Now, I told you . . . .

ROGERS: Damn it. Keep your voice down.

TAYLOR: All right, but nothing risky. I don't want to get shot.

ROGERS: I think I know how to get past the knights.

JENKINS: The knights?

ROGERS: I'm sorry. I mean the guards. Look, if we can get Gates alone, we can get control of this island. Right?

TAYLOR: Now wait a minute . . . .

ROGERS: Listen first. What happens every time Gates comes in this room?

TAYLOR: You mean the dummy with the rifle?

ROGERS: Yes, Mute. He's up there on the balcony. covering us all with the rifle. Then he disappears when Donne gives him a signal.

TAYLOR: If you think I'm going to jump that character, you got another think coming. He'd like to kill me.

ROGERS: You won't have to worry about Mute. You won't have to go near him.

TAYLOR: Good, that suits me good.

ROGERS: You grab Gates.

TAYLOR: Hell, no.

ROGERS: Keep your voice down. Why not?

TAYLOR: I'd just never get the chance, that's why not. Anybody try to jump Gates would get it both ways— from the dummy and from Donne.

JENKINS: Shut up, Taylor. Go on, Rogers, you've thought of a way to get them both out of the way, haven't you?

TAYLOR: I don't even want to hear about it. If Gates wants to shoot somebody, it's all right with me. He can shoot Jenkins' brown girl friend; it's all right with me, but I ain't going to get killed.

JENKINS: Damn you, Taylor, and your foul mouth. I'll break your filthy neck.

ROGERS: Let's not start fighting among ourselves. That's exactly what Gates wants.

JENKINS: I'm sorry, Rogers, but this ... this ... .

ROGERS: I think this plan has a chance. Will you try it?

JENKINS: I'll try anything.

TAYLOR: Well, I won't.

JENKINS: Taylor, you get my next vote.

TAYLOR: I can tell Gates. I'll tell him you're ganging up on me because I wouldn't help you.

JENKINS: He doesn't give a damn. He just wants a victim, and if you don't go with us, Taylor, you're going to be it. I mean it, Taylor. If you have any idea that you're going to load this on any of us — any *one* of us—it won't work. Nobody likes you anyway.

TAYLOR: I know that. I know that. I knew you'd gang up on me sooner or later. I knew it all along. It's always like that.

ROGERS: Nobody's ganging up on you, Taylor.

TAYLOR: Hell, you're not. You said you'd vote for me. Now he's going to vote for me, and probably that colored girl too. That's three votes—three out of seven. One more and I'm the pigeon. Don't tell me you're not ganging up on me. I've been ganged up on before. I know.

ROGERS: Keep your voice down. My plan is to save all seven of us —not six. Do you want to hear it?

TAYLOR: I ain't got any choice, have I?

ROGERS: Look at this door and think about what Gates does every time he comes in.

JENKINS: I think I'd better go and get Loretta ... Miss Grant.

ROGERS: We don't need the women in this.

JENKINS: I left her alone there ... down by the sea wall.

ROGERS: She's safe. No one will bother her. Now, let's ... .

JENKINS: I'm worried about her. She can't see since that damned Gates broke her glasses.

TAYLOR: She's got that cane he gave her, ain't she?

JENKINS: I'm telling you, Taylor, more and more, I'd just like to vote for you and the hell with everything else.

ROGERS: She'll be all right. She's been going around without glasses for two weeks. She knows this place now.

TAYLOR: I didn't mean nothing.

ROGERS: *(Going to the doors, followed by the others)* Look, when Gates comes in, he is followed by Donne. But he doesn't like anybody near him, so it's always ten or fifteen seconds after he's in the room before Donne gets in. When Gates gets in the room, we'll slam the door and put the chair against it. Then you grab Gates, Taylor.

TAYLOR: And get shot. Hell no.

ROGERS: Shut up and listen to me. You won't get shot. We got Gates inside and Donne outside. Donne can't shoot you.

TAYLOR: But that dummy up there can. Right in the face. Hell, I'd rather get shot in the back than in the face.

ROGERS: He can't shoot you unless he sees you.

TAYLOR: Why won't he see me? He's dumb, not blind.

ROGERS: He won't see you because it will be dark. As soon as that door opens, Jenkins will pull the switch, and you'll pull Gates into the dark. We'll have him before Mute can even know what's happening.

TAYLOR: I ain't sure I can hold him. He might get away.

JENKINS: You'd better make sure he doesn't. Hell,

can't you even grab a crippled man?

TAYLOR: Sure. Sure. *(Turns downstage)* I'm supposed to make sure. I ain't no fighter. I never said I was. Gates may be a lot stronger than he looks. Being crippled don't mean he ain't strong. I don't like it. I don't think I can hold him.

ROGERS: You've got to.

JENKINS: Let me do the grabbing, and Taylor can get the lights.

ROGERS: No.

TAYLOR: Why not? Why not? That sounds fine to me.

ROGERS: Two reasons. One, I want Gates alive, and you hate him too much, Jenkins.

JENKINS: I'll keep him alive. For now.

ROGERS: And I want you to be alive, too.

TAYLOR: But you don't care about me, is that it?

ROGERS: No, *that's* not it. I want to be sure those lights go out. You, Taylor, may decide not to turn them out.

TAYLOR: Hell, why would I do a thing like that?

ROGERS: I don't know. I don't know why you decided to change your vote today either.

TAYLOR: I didn't do any . . . .

ROGERS: Gates told me.

TAYLOR: You're lying. He didn't have no business doing that.

JENKINS: How did you vote, Taylor?

ROGERS: It's not important. Duke will help us, won't
you, Duke?

TAYLOR: I guess so. Yeah, I'll help you. But I'm not
just going to grab him. I'm going to grab that
damned cane of his and give him a lump on the
head. I'm going to knock him out. He had no business telling on me.

ROGERS: We want Gates alive, Taylor, you hear me?

JENKINS: Might be better if he did knock him out. He
won't kill him. Gates has got a thick head.

ROGERS: All right. You grab him and knock him out.
But be careful. We're in a lot better position if
we've got him alive.

JENKINS: What do we do after we get him?

TAYLOR: *If* we get him.

ROGERS: That will be up to Mr. Gates. But once we
have him, the others won't be a problem. The rest
of the pieces don't make any difference when you

get the King.

JENKINS: All right. You think we should try it once?

ROGERS: Jenkins, you be Gates. Go outside, and Duke and I will be ready for you. We'll leave the lights on. We don't want to make Mute suspicious.

JENKINS: All right, I'll go out. *(Starts to open doors)*

ROGERS: And, Taylor, you just grab him. Don't hit him.

TAYLOR: I'd sure like to.

The three men go to their positions. TAYLOR stands by the door so that as soon as it opens, he can grab JENKINS. ROGERS takes a chair and stands in a position so that he can slam the door quickly and put the chair in position under the handle. JENKINS goes out the door. Both TAYLOR and ROGERS are now out of view of the balcony. MUTE comes out and looks, sees the room empty, and returns up the stairs. He has not seen TAYLOR or ROGERS, and they have not seen him.

ROGERS: *(Quietly to TAYLOR)* Remember, just grab him.

JENKINS opens the door, TAYLOR grabs him, pulls him into the room and holds him by wrapping his arm around his neck. ROG-

*ERS sets the chair under the knob and tries
the door. It holds. He removes the chair.*

JENKINS: *(Shaking loose from TAYLOR)* You don't
have to choke the life out of me.

TAYLOR: You want me to do a good job, don't you?

JENKINS: What do we do now?

ROGERS: Now, we just wait.

TAYLOR: Maybe I ought to get some kind of club I can
hit him with. *(Picks up a heavy bookend)* This
ought to do it.

ROGERS: You'll kill him with that.

TAYLOR: I'll just tap him.

ROGERS: If Miss Britt or one of the others comes in
first, we'll just have to put this off.

JENKINS: When I was out in the hall, I saw Gates and
Donne coming up from the beach. They'll be here
soon.

ROGERS: Let's not talk anymore.

JENKINS: Wait a minute. Where's the light switch.

ROGERS: Damn it. I forgot. *(Showing him)* It's here.

JENKINS: Maybe I should try it.

ROGERS: You don't need to try it. I tried it just before
you came in.

The three stand nervously.

TAYLOR: Maybe we ought to wait until tomorrow night.

ROGERS: It's now, or we'll never do it.

*The stage lights dim, and the clicking of a
cane in the hall beyond the doors can be
heard.*

ROGERS: It's Gates. Get ready.

*The door starts to open; the lights go out,
and the three men follow out their plan.*

ROGERS: Now.

TAYLOR: I got him. Get that damned door.

There's banging at the door and confusion.

JENKINS: Have you got him, Taylor?

TAYLOR: He's out. He's out. I knocked him out.

GATES: *(Outside the door)* What's going on in there?
Why is this door locked?

JENKINS: He's outside. Gates is outside.

ROGERS: Turn on the lights.

JENKINS: Damn you, Taylor, you said you had him.

The lights come on and TAYLOR is kneeling over the body of LORETTA GRANT.

JENKINS: It's Loretta. You ... you ...

He goes to her body and kneels; TAYLOR moves back.

God, what have you done?

TAYLOR: I thought it was .....

He looks up at the balcony, sees MUTE, who is standing there with the rifle, and backs away from the rifle.

TAYLOR: No, no, don't shoot. It's not him.

JENKINS: What have you done? What have you done? She's dead.

ROGERS: Oh. God, what have I done?

GATES: Open the door. Open the door in there. *(He continues banging on the door)*

CURTAIN

ACT TWO

The same scene, two hours later. The curtains in front of the French doors are pulled together.

As the curtain rises, GATES is sitting on the chair upstage left. MRS. CLYME is standing next to his chair. MUTE is standing guard on the balcony: DONNE is standing behind Gates' chair. The lonely appear to be almost paralyzed. SABRE DAWSON and FAYE ALLEN are sitting on the sofa, stage right, close together. MISS BRITT and TAYLOR are sitting on the upstage sofa, the sofa length apart. JENKINS is sitting on the downstage left chair: and ROGERS is standing downstage left, looking out of a "window" in the fourth wall.

GATES: It was a stupid move to make. Stupid. I really expected more of you, Mr. Rogers. I really did.

TAYLOR: I didn't mean to kill anybody. I didn't hit her that hard.

JENKINS: You must have known it was a woman. The moment you touched her, you must have known.

TAYLOR: It happened so fast. I just saw the cane and thought it was Mr. Gates. I didn't do it on purpose. You didn't know it was a woman until we turned on the lights. Why blame me?

72

JENKINS: I didn't touch her. You knew. You're the one who voted against her. If it takes me the rest of my life, I'll get you, Taylor.

GATES: Please, no malice. After all, I was the one you all intended to kill, and I bear you no malice. I am a little dismayed, perhaps, to think that my guests should behave in such a manner. But I bear no one any malice.

TAYLOR: I didn't intend to kill you, Mr. Gates. Just knock you out a little.

GATES: Oh, just knock me out a little? Why, thank you, Duke. It is so nice just to be knocked out a little.

BRITT: Mrs. Clyme, would you mind bringing me a glass of ...?

GATES: Not now, Miss Britt. Perhaps later when we finish our business.

BRITT: I just wanted a glass of water. A small glass of water.

GATES: Not now, Miss Britt.

BRITT: I'm thirsty. Very thirsty.

GATES: All right. Mrs. Clyme, please get Miss Britt a glass of water.

MRS. CLYME exits through upstage center doors, closing the doors behind her.

We are going to vote now.

BRITT: There's already been one vote today.

GATES: Things have changed. We are going to vote again now. And this time it will be a voice vote.

BRITT: It doesn't seem fair. You said .....

GATES: I didn't make laws myself to bind. It's too bad Miss Grant isn't here. She was a scholar, a teacher, and would understand my reference. *(Rises and moves downstage)* But, Miss Grant, isn't here, alas. Mr. Rogers, how are you voting?

ROGERS doesn't move.

Mr. Rogers, what do you find so interesting out of the window? The sea?

ROGERS: No. Not the sea. I'm just looking.

GATES: Looking at nothing? You must be bored. Perhaps, you are ready to vote then, Mr. Rogers.

ROGERS: I'm not voting.

GATES: Come, Mr. Rogers, you are not being very cooperative. You had plenty of ideas a few hours ago. Life was a great chess game then, wasn't it? And you were the master chess player, going to

74

take the King with a trio of pawns. Have you lost your imagination, Mr. Rogers?

ROGERS: Yes. Yes, I've lost my imagination.

GATES: After all, it isn't your fault that the Grant girl is dead. That wasn't your fault.

ROGERS: I didn't say it was.

GATES: No one blames you. Even Mr. Jenkins doesn't blame you. He blames Taylor, don't you, Mr. Jenkins? Now if you would blame Taylor, Mr. Taylor would be in a fair way of ... of winning the election.

TAYLOR: Hey, what are you trying to do to me?

GATES: Don't worry, Mr. Taylor. Mr. Rogers doesn't blame you. He blames himself. Or perhaps he blames me. When people don't want to blame themselves, they blame me. But it's all one.

ROGERS: Just what is it you want?

GATES: I want your cooperation. I want you to vote.

ROGERS: I'm not going to vote.

GATES: That will never do, Mr. Rogers. You are going to vote. If not now, an hour from now.

DAWSON: We're not going to keep this up for an hour, are we? God, I'll go crazy.

GATES: You see, Mr. Rogers. You see what you are causing now.

ROGERS: All right, I'll vote. I vote for myself.

GATES: Mr. Rogers, you don't look well. Would you like to go out on the patio for a breath of fresh air? The sea is lovely tonight. Dark and inviting.

ROGERS: No. No, thank you. Not now. I'm all right.

GATES: As you please, Mr. Rogers, but you don't want to push yourself too hard. Isn't that what your mother used to say, Mr. Rogers?

ROGERS: If only hate killed others . . . .

GATES: Your hate would kill me? It doesn't work that way, Mr. Rogers. Not quite that way. But you may stand there and think about it. *(To OTHERS)* Well, we have one vote. Mr. Jenkins, would you care to make it two?

JENKINS: Taylor. I vote for Taylor.

ROGERS: Don't do it, Jenkins. Don't do it.

JENKINS: I don't need any more ideas from you. If you had listened to me, we'd have all voted for Taylor in the first place. I vote for Taylor.

GATES: One vote for Taylor. All right.

TAYLOR: I vote for Jenkins. You can put that down,

too. Two can play the same game, Jenkins.

GATES: Now, we have three candidates. And all fine upstanging gentlemen, whole men. Miss Britt, you're next.

BRITT: I'm not voting. I'm not voting for anyone. I'm just not.

GATES: You may do as you please, of course. You are my guest. But I should note, Miss Britt, that the bar is closed until the election is over. That's the law every place, and we must obey the law.

BRITT: I ... I don't care. I'm not voting.

MRS. CLYME comes in and gives MISS BRITT a small glass of water. MISS BRITT sips it, then tastes it, then takes a larger gulp. She smiles at MRS. CLYME who takes no notice, but returns to her position behind GATES.

GATES: After all, Miss Britt, you shared a room with Miss Grant. Somebody is responsible for her death. You do owe her something.

BRITT: Miss Grant wouldn't want me to. She wouldn't want me to hurt anyone here. She was a gentle person. I never heard her say anything about anyone.

GATES: Oh, come now. She hated me, didn't she?

BRITT: You were insulting to her. But I don't think she really hated you. Not really.

GATES: You're wrong, Miss Britt. You are wrong. *(Vehemently)* She hated me.

BRITT: She was a gentle person. I'm not going to vote. *(She sips from her glass)*

GATES: *(Going to MISS BRITT, taking glass, and sniffing it)* Mrs. Clyme, one of these times you will interfere once too often. You are not immune, you know. *(Hands glass back to MISS BRITT)* Sip your water, Miss Britt. Sip it and think. I'll return to you. *(Turns downstage toward MRS. ALLEN and MISS DAWSON)* Mrs. Allen?

The two women continue to stare ahead of them, taking no notice of him.

Mrs. Allen, it is your vote.

JENKINS: Leave the women out of it. We got enough votes now. You let me kill Taylor, and I don't care what you do to me.

GATES: That's a barbaric idea, Jenkins. Tempting, I'll admit, but barbaric. Mrs. Allen, what do you think of the idea?

ALLEN: *(Without looking at him or anyone)* I vote for Taylor.

GATES: Oh?

78

TAYLOR: I knew she would. I saw the way she was
looking at him.

GATES: Mr. Taylor, please don't interrupt. And now,
Miss Dawson?

DAWSON: I vote for Jenkins.

ROGERS: Good God, stop it. Stop it. Stop it. Don't you
see what he's doing? He's trying to make us kill
each other.

GATES: Mr. Rogers, the only killing done around here
was your business. You've had your vote; now let
the others have theirs.

ROGERS: God, you're diseased.

GATES: If all this is distasteful to you, Mr. Rogers
. . . .

ROGERS: I'm sick.

GATES: You need a breath of fresh air, Mr. Rogers.

ROGERS: Yes, fresh air. *(Starts for patio, then
stops)* I know what I'm doing, Gates.

GATES: I'm sure you do.

> *ROGERS goes to French doors, pulls back
> the curtain, opens the door, and goes out on
> the patio. GATES nods to DONNE, who fol-
> lows ROGERS, closes the patio door, and*

stands there looking out.

GATES: I do hope Mr. Rogers isn't going to be deathly ill. He's such a nice man. Would any of you care to join him? I should warn you that he's sometimes violent. Do you know that he almost killed his own mother because she tried to stop him ... but there's no need to gossip. And I'm sure he meant her no harm. Miss Dawson, do I hear you correctly?

DAWSON: I voted for Jenkins.

TAYLOR: *(Laughing)* I knew she would. We're still even, Jenkins.

ALLEN: *(Who has stared at DAWSON from the moment she voted, rises and crosses the stage to the position ROGERS has left)* I just love the sea at night, don't you, Mr. Jenkins?

DAWSON: *(Almost screaming)* Faye.

ALLEN: Maybe later, we could walk along the sea wall together, Mr. Jenkins.

DAWSON: Faye, please, don't.

ALLEN: *(Turning toward her)* Did you speak to me?

DAWSON: Faye, what's the matter with you?

ALLEN: Anyone who would vote against a nice gentleman like Mr. Jenkins for a man like Taylor ...

well, she's just no friend of mine. *(Turns toward JENKINS)* There's a moon tonight, Billy Joe.

GATES: Has there been a misunderstanding? Miss Dawson, would you like to change your vote?

DAWSON: No. No, I wouldn't. *(Almost whispering)* I'll never change my vote now.

TAYLOR: I'll change mine. I'll vote for Miss Dawson.

ALLEN: Yes. I'll vote for Miss Dawson, too.

TAYLOR: I knew it. I knew she would. Now it's two for Miss Dawson, one for Jenkins, one for Mr. Rogers, and one for me. You've got somebody. You don't need us.

GATES: Very shrewd, Mr. Taylor. I now see how you have managed to live so long. Miss Dawson, would you like to reconsider?

DAWSON: *(Looks at MRS. ALLEN, who looks away)* No.

GATES: Mrs. Allen?

MRS. ALLEN merely shakes her head.

JENKINS: Taylor, you listen to me. You think you're getting away with something, but you're not. If we both get away from here alive, I'm going to find you and I'm going to kill you. If it takes me the rest of my life, I'm going to kill you.

GATES: Well, Mr. Taylor, now would you care to change your vote?

TAYLOR: He don't scare me. He can talk and talk and talk. But he won't find me. If I get away from here, nobody will ever find me again.

GATES: Well, so be it.

He turns upstage to MISS BRITT, who has been sitting quietly removed, sipping her drink slowly.

Well, Miss Britt, that leaves only you. You'll have to vote now. Just think, Miss Britt, if you refuse to vote, Miss Dawson will have won tonight's election.

BRITT: I'm not going to vote. I'm not even going to say anything about it.

GATES: I thought you liked Miss Dawson. She's rather like you—twenty years ago or so, of course.

BRITT: I'm not going to say anything about it. I'm not listening.

JENKINS: Call Rogers in. He'll vote for Taylor. He knows that Taylor killed Loretta on purpose. *(He rises as though to go for ROGERS.)*

There is a dying scream from ROGERS on the patio.

GATES: Mr. Rogers has, I believe, taken his leave of us. Would you see if he made it, Donne?

DONNE opens the French doors: the wind blows the curtain. He steps out on the patio, out of sight. The others sit tensely, waiting.

GATES: I don't suppose he could have made a mistake this time. It's over three hundred feet straight down.

JENKINS: You sent him out there to do it. You sent him out there to jump. I wish the hell he had thrown you off instead.

GATES: You knew that's what he was going out there for, Mr. Jenkins. All of you knew. I asked if any of you wanted to help him. No one volunteered.

There is silence.

You don't need to blame yourselves. He has been wanting to do that for a long time. He just never had exactly the right setting before.

JENKINS: You're a bastard. A lousy, crummy bastard.

GATES: Mr. Jenkins. I had hoped that I would never have to lecture my guests on their manners.

JENKINS: I'm not your damned guest. I'm your prisoner.

GATES: And there are ladies present. I've always felt that violent language really came from men who weren't quite sure of their manliness. Are you worried about your manliness, Mr. Jenkins?

JENKINS: *(Being drained of all rational anger)* You're a .... I don't know what you are. *(Sits)* I don't know anything. But I'm through trying. I'm through. You can kill me if you like, but I'm through.

GATES: Well, then, good. Shall we get down to business.

DONNE: *(Who has returned and closed the French doors)* He missed the sea and hit the rocks. I'll get him in the morning.

GATES: It's too bad. He would have liked the sea. Well, Miss Britt, have you changed your mind now?

CURTAIN

ACT THREE

SCENE 1: It is two weeks later, the last night of the game. The stage is empty, but SABRE DAWSON is on the patio. MRS. ALLEN enters and looks about, sees no one, and sits down on the downstage left chair, picks up a book there and starts to leaf through it. JEN- KINS comes down the stairs, and MRS. AL- LEN rises.

ALLEN: Hello.

JENKINS: *(Trying not to look at her)* Hello.

ALLEN: I didn't see you this afternoon.

JENKINS: I went down to the ... down to the place where he buried them.

ALLEN: I would have gone with you.

JENKINS: I wanted to go alone.

ALLEN: *(Going toward him)* You're tired of me, aren't you? Just a week, and already you're tired of me. You can tell me, Billy.

JENKINS: It's not that.

ALLEN: You didn't mean those things you said. You're not going to take me with you, are you?

JENKINS: I can't. I thought I could, but I can't. You need somebody to take care of you. I can't take care of anyone, not even myself.

ALLEN: Do you want me to go with her?

JENKINS: I don't want you to, no.

ALLEN: But you're not going to stop me, are you?

JENKINS: I can't. I don't know how.

ALLEN: We're going to vote pretty soon. And this is the last time. If I voted for you, Taylor would too.

JENKINS: Yes, I know.

ALLEN: You wouldn't want me to do that, would you?

JENKINS: I'm sorry, Faye. But I don't care what you do .... .

He turns and goes out the upstage center doors.

ALLEN: Wait. Billy Joe, wait. I wouldn't do .... . I wouldn't do anything like that to you.

The door closes behind him.

I'd rather vote for me than you. Honest, I would.

MISS DAWSON has come on stage from the patio.

DAWSON: He's walking out on you, isn't he? I knew he would. Now, I suppose you want to come crawling back to me. Well?

ALLEN: *(Turning toward her)* You were there all the time, weren't you? There, spying on me?

DAWSON: I was watching the sea. I didn't even know you were here until I heard you and your boyfriend screaming at each other. I don't know what I could have done then except jump in the sea. You'd have liked that, wouldn't you? You'd like it if I jumped in the sea.

ALLEN: Yes, I would. I'd like to see you fall down. I'd like to see your body hit the rocks. I'd like to hear you scream.

DAWSON: You don't mean all those things, Faye. *(Starts toward her)* Faye, I ... I'm your friend. I'll take care of you.

ALLEN: *(Drawing back)* Stay away from me. I don't want anything to do with you. You just want me to vote for somebody else. Well, I'm not going to.

DAWSON: You can vote for me if you want to. I don't care if I die or not. You want me to jump into the sea? *(Starts to turn back toward the patio)* You want to hear me scream? I'll do it.

She starts for the patio, but MRS. ALLEN steps ahead of her and closes the French doors.

ALLEN: No. No. I don't want anyone to die. I don't know what's happening to us. *(Walks downstage)* We were kind of happy when we were together first, in the desert. It wasn't even so bad the first week here. But then the girl was killed, ... then you turned against me .....

DAWSON: You turned against me.

ALLEN: Then Mr. Rogers ... did that to himself. And then Billy Joe .... . And now, I'm trying to kill you. We're all crazy.

DAWSON: It will be all right when we get away.

ALLEN: It won't be all right. We'll always know that the first time something happens, we'll .... . The only one who hasn't changed is Miss Britt. She's the only one.

DAWSON: How could she? She's drunk all the time. Oh, you'll see, Faye. When we get away, everything will be all right. I know it will.

ALLEN: I don't think we're going to get away. None of us. I think this is the last night for all of us.

DAWSON: Mr. Gates said that tomorrow we could all go home.

ALLEN: He doesn't mean it.

DAWSON: He means it, Faye. He must mean it. If he just wanted to kill us, he could do that. He wouldn't need all this.

ALLEN: He doesn't want to kill us. He wants us to kill ourselves. And we'll do it, too. We'll do it. You wait.

DAWSON: No, we won't. We'll all vote for Jenkins. Then he'll let the rest of us go.

ALLEN: No.

DAWSON: He walked away from you. He deserted you.

ALLEN: I don't care.

DAWSON: It won't do you any good. He'll never look at you again. I know men, Faye. I know them. He'll never look at you again.

ALLEN: I don't care. I don't want him to. But I'm not going to kill him. I'm not going to kill anyone.

DAWSON: All right. All right. Then we'll vote for Taylor. He ought to die anyway. He killed that girl. And he meant to do it. I know he meant to. He hated her, and she never did a thing to him.

MISS BRITT starts down the stairs.

ALLEN: I'm not going to kill anyone.

BRITT: Has anyone seen Mrs. Clyme? She promised to fix me a little drink.

*MRS. ALLEN and MISS DAWSON look at
MISS BRITT, and then without answering,
they both sit down.*

BRITT: *(Sitting down on upstage-center sofa)* I just
asked.

ALLEN: I haven't seen her, Miss Britt.

BRITT: Thank you. *(Pauses)* I sort of like Mrs.
Clyme. Of course, I know she's with that man.
But I don't think she can help it. She's been very
nice to me.

There is no answer.

I wonder where the others are? I guess Mr. Gates
will be here soon.

TAYLOR starts down the stairs.

I guess he wouldn't let me have a little drink first
anyway. But I don't care. I'm not going to say a
single word about that anyway. Everybody can do
what he likes, but I'm not going to take part.

*TAYLOR comes down and sits down next to
MISS BRITT.*

I'm not going to take part.

TAYLOR: Isn't anyone going to speak to me?

BRITT: Good evening.

TAYLOR: I haven't got anything against anybody. But a man's got to look out for himself. You can see that, can't you, Miss Dawson?

DAWSON: I'd rather you wouldn't talk to me.

TAYLOR: All right. I can see where you wouldn't like me. I can see it. But you ought to see my position, too. I've got to live, too, haven't I?

ALLEN: Why? Why have you got to live too?

TAYLOR: So that's the way it's going to go, is it? Damned women. A man's dead if he counts on a woman. He's dead.

The upstage center doors open, JENKINS enters, followed by GATES and DONNE. MUTE appears on the balcony. MRS. ALLEN looks up at him.

ALLEN: That's very neat. It really is. Every time you appear, Mr. Gates, out jumps the little man with a gun. When I was a girl, I had a little thing that I hung on the wall. When it was going to rain, a little figure came out, carrying an umbrella.

GATES: That's very poetic, Mrs. Allen.

JENKINS walks downstage to the left side and appears to be staring out.

Very poetic.

He observes MRS. ALLEN watching JEN-KINS.

GATES: Don't you think that's very poetic, Mr. Jenkins?

JENKINS doesn't answer.

Well, it is. It's very poetic, Mrs. Allen.

MRS. CLYME enters from upstage center door. She is a little flushed, and she carries a glass.

CLYME: Has the voting started yet?

GATES: No, not yet. *(Looking at glass)* What's that?

CLYME: Just medicine. Some medicine for Miss Britt.

GATES: You know I don't approve of this, Mrs. Clyme.

CLYME: May I give it to her?

GATES shrugs, and MRS. CLYME carries the drink to MISS BRITT.

TAYLOR: I could stand a little shot of that myself.

GATES: This is the last night. Tomorrow, all of you— save one—will return home. But ...

BRITT: I'm not going to say anything about that. I'm not going to name anybody.

GATES: *(Ignoring her)* But we must still vote. Now, where shall we start? Duke, how about you?

TAYLOR: I don't want to vote now.

GATES: Oh? I had thought sure that Miss Dawson had your vote. I see there has been a change. Well, we'll return to you. How about you, Mr. Jenkins?

JENKINS appears not to hear.

I must say you are not very cooperative tonight. Mr. Jenkins, it is your vote.

JENKINS still does not respond.

Well, we shall return to you later, too. Miss Dawson, it appears that the honor of casting the first vote goes to you.

DAWSON: *(Looks at MRS. ALLEN, then looks down)* Taylor.

GATES: Taylor. Well. This is interesting. We now have a vote. And, Mrs. Allen? What is your vote?

ALLEN: I'm not going to vote.

GATES: Mrs. Allen, we don't have much time. You are all leaving in the morning, and you have packing to do, good-byes to make. *(Sits down)* I'm not really sure I know what to do. Mrs. Clyme, do you have a suggestion?

CLYME: Since they have all had an opportunity to vote, you could simply elect the one who got the most votes.

GATES: Do you think that's really fair? After all, one vote. There really should be six votes at least. I always hope for seven, you know. But now there are only five, and Duke does not seem likely to vote for himself. So the best could be four. I'd even settle for three. But one. I don't know. That does seem pretty thin.

TAYLOR: I'm ready to vote now. I still have a chance. I want to vote.

GATES: Well, I don't know. What do you think, Mrs. Clyme?

CLYME: It's only fair, I guess. Let him vote.

TAYLOR: That's right. It's only fair. I vote for Jenkins.

GATES: Jenkins. All right. That's one vote each. Well, now, Mr. Jenkins, would you like to make your vote?

JENKINS does not move.

No. Well, that seems to be it. Perhaps, we'll have to have two this time. They each have one vote, so
. . . .

ALLEN: I vote for Taylor.

JENKINS turns toward her, but she stares straight ahead.

I vote for Taylor.

GATES: Well, Duke, you again have two votes, and Mr. Jenkins has one vote. You are the winner, it appears.

TAYLOR: *(Rising now, in anger)* I could have told you. I could have told you that right from the beginning. I knew those damned women would do it to me. *(Starts toward JENKINS)* You don't have to kill me now, do you, Jenkins? You can let your damned women do it for you. You're a great one, boy. A real great one. You get them all. Every age and every color. I don't know what you got, boy, but it's something.

JENKINS: *(Turns, grabs a bookend from the end-table and starts toward him)* Damn you. I'm going to kill you.

He races toward TAYLOR, who stumbles back and falls. MUTE raises his rifle and fires from the balcony, and JENKINS drops, shot through the heart.

TAYLOR: *(Stumbling to his feet, and drawing back)* He would have killed me. He really would have.

GATES: *(To MUTE)* You stupid animal. You inter-
fered.

DONNE: You told him if any of them started anything,
he was to shoot. He was just doing what he was
told.

GATES: Well, it can't be helped now.

ALLEN: He's dead. He just shot him. He's dead. Isn't
anybody going to do anything for him? At least
look at him?

GATES: Why don't you, Mrs. Allen? He was *your* lov-
er.

ALLEN: I ... I can't.

*She turns away, facing toward the French
doors, and covers her face. DAWSON goes
to her.*

DAWSON: It's all right, Faye. It's all right, Honey.
I'll take care of you. *(Turns to GATES)* Can we
go to our room now? Can we leave?

BRITT: He was a nice young man. He was a nice young
man. I'm not going to say anything.

DAWSON: Can we leave now?

GATES: We should have another vote.

DAWSON: Three are dead now. Isn't that enough? Isn't there an end anyplace?

GATES: It will end tomorrow, just as I promised. But first we have to vote.

ALLEN: No. No. No. No more. No more. I can't breathe.

DAWSON: Faye. Faye, darling. *(To GATES)* We're leaving. We're going to our room. If you want to have us killed, go ahead. We don't care.

MISS DAWSON leads MRS. ALLEN toward the stairs.

GATES: Oh, very well. We can have the vote tomorrow morning. Just before you all leave. I do like to be reasonable about these things. *(To DONNE)* Take poor Mr. Jenkins out of here. He looks most depressing there on the floor. Most depressing.

CURTAIN

ACT THREE

*SCENE 2: It is the next morning. The French
doors are open, and the room is bathed in
sunlight. Bouquets of flowers are spotted
around the room. MRS. CLYME is arrang-
ing one. GATES is standing by the French
doors, and the sea now sounds quiet and
restful, almost pleasant. MISS BRITT,
dressed as if to go to market, is sitting on
the upstage-center sofa, her suitcase in
front of her. MISS DAWSON and MRS. AL-
LEN are seated on the sofa, stage right,
their suitcases by them. They sit like
strangers in a bus depot, waiting for an an-
nouncement of their departure. DONNE
stands by the door of the study.*

GATES: *(Looking out the doors)* The sea is calm this
morning, almost as if a storm had passed. It will
be a good day to travel.

CLYME: Do these flowers look all right, Mr. Gates?

GATES: *(Without looking at them)* Very nice, Mrs.
Clyme. Very nice.

CLYME: I do like things to look nice the last morning.
Last impressions are so comforting.

GATES: Yes, yes, very nice. *(Turns toward room)*
I wish that we could have taken care of all this bus-

iness last night. I am really very tired of the whole business. Very tired.

CLYME: I know, Mr. Gates. I know. Just a little longer.

GATES: I almost feel like just junking the whole business. I really don't know why I should go on.

CLYME: There doesn't seem to be much point to it now. There really doesn't.

GATES: If people would just behave with some sort of decency. Just think, six would be leaving now. Six happy people. But no, we had to have all that dreadful business. Well, I suppose it was better done here than out there. Society owes us much.

CLYME: I suppose, but no one even admits we are here.

GATES: But still we must go on.

TAYLOR appears on the balcony and starts down the stairs. He wears his hat. MUTE follows him, carrying his rifle.

GATES: Duke, haven't you forgotten your suitcase?

TAYLOR: It ain't mine. It's yours.

GATES: But I gave it to you.

TAYLOR: I don't want it. *(He has now reached the*

room and he looks about him) Looks like a damned funeral.

CLYME: That's not a nice thing to say.

GATES: No, Duke, it isn't.

TAYLOR: *(Shakes his head, half-laughing)* You two are the damndest people. You kidnap us, set us against each other, kill us. And I ain't supposed to say it looks like a funeral. Well, pardon me, but I'll say it if I feel like it. It's my funeral.

He goes to sit down on sofa with MISS BRITT.

Good morning, Miss Britt.

BRITT: Good morning, Mr. Taylor.

GATES: Well, I'm glad we're all being so reasonable this morning. Perhaps we can get down to business.

CLYME: Miss Britt, may I get you a little something?

BRITT: No thank you. I'm not thirsty.

CLYME: If you change your mind, you let me know.

GATES: Mrs. Clyme, I'm afraid you're not objective. You've shown your preference for Miss Britt from the day she arrived.

CLYME: Well, we all have our favorites, Mr. Gates.

100

You were most partial to Mr. Rogers. And it showed. Don't think it didn't.

GATES: There's no need to quarrel about it. *(Turns from her)* Well, shall we have our vote?

TAYLOR: There's no sense in that. I'm picked and I know it. I knew it from the beginning, but at least it wasn't just me. I don't go alone. I'll have some company out there on that beach. But don't bury me next to that colored girl, that's all I ask. Don't bury me next to that colored girl.

GATES: Please, Duke. Let's go about this properly. First, we vote. Would you like to vote first, Duke?

TAYLOR: Why the hell not? I cast my vote for Jason Taylor. Jason Taylor, that's me. That's my name. Not Duke. Jason. None of you knew that, did you? Don't make any difference. I vote for Jason Taylor, the Duke of Nothing. I might as well get all four. I won't be any deader.

GATES: Miss Britt, are you going to vote this time? It's your last chance.

BRITT: Yes, it is, isn't it? I'm going to vote. I'll vote for myself, too.

DAWSON: We're not going to start that again. Voting, changing votes, and then somebody dies. If you're going to kill us, Mr. Gates, kill us all now and be done with it.

GATES: Are you ready to vote, Miss Dawson?

DAWSON: I .... No, I'm not going to vote.

BRITT: Please, Miss Dawson, vote for me.

DAWSON: What?

BRITT: Vote for me. You're right. Mr. Gates wants us to keep killing each other, but if you'll all vote for me, it will be all over.

DAWSON: We can't do that.

BRITT: Why not? Do you want to die, Miss Dawson?

DAWSON starts to answer, but then looks down silently.

BRITT: And you, Mrs. Allen, do you want to die?

MRS. ALLEN does not answer.

And I know you don't, Duke.

TAYLOR: I don't. I sure don't. That's the truth. But I don't want you dying, either. I ain't got anything against you, Miss Britt.

BRITT: No one has, Duke. No one ever has. None of you want to die.

TAYLOR: You don't either. Do you?

BRITT: No. No, I don't. Not really. But I don't really care. I don't want to go back home. There's no Mrs. Clyme there to bring me medicine. *(Smiles at MRS. CLYME)* And just think, Mrs. Clyme, you can come visit my grave and pour spirits on it.

CLYME: Yes, Miss Britt, I'll do that. And I'll bring flowers, too.

BRITT: You see, it's all settled. Mrs. Clyme wants me to stay.

DAWSON: I'm not going to do it. I'm not going to pick you.

ALLEN: I'm not either.

BRITT: That's all right. Duke will vote for me. Won't you, Duke?

TAYLOR: I ... *(Looks away)* Well, if that's what you want. If you're sure that's what you want.

BRITT: Well, Mrs. Clyme, you see you were right.

CLYME: Shall I get you something to drink?

BRITT: No. No, I don't need anything to drink for this. *(Looks from MUTE to DONNE)* Well, which one of you is to have the honor?

DONNE: *(Looks at GATES who nods)* If you'll come with me, Miss Britt.

He indicates she is to go to the upstage center doors.

BRITT: Will it ... ? Does it ... ?

DONNE: It doesn't hurt.

BRITT: Of course, you'd have no real way of knowing, would you? *(Turns back to the room)* Good-bye, everybody.

No one answers her, but GATES and MRS. CLYME look at her, almost fondly.

You won't forget to sprinkle my grave, Mrs. Clyme?

CLYME: I won't forget. And I'll remember the flowers, too. Rosemary, for remembrance.

BRITT: Thank you. And pansies, too. That's for thought, isn't it, Mr. Gates?

She exits through the door, and DONNE follows her.

GATES: Well, the rest of you are now free to leave. The boat is ready.

TAYLOR: You mean it? You really mean it?

GATES: I mean it.

ALLEN: Shouldn't we wait a minute until ... ?

GATES: You won't see her anymore.

TAYLOR: *(Standing)* I'm really going, eh, alive?

GATES: You really are, Duke. *(To MUTE)* Mute, take our guests to the boat and start them on their way home.

They rise. DAWSON and MRS. ALLEN look at each other and start toward upstage center door, MUTE falls in behind them. TAYLOR gets up, then stops.

TAYLOR: I guess I'd better get my suitcase then. I mean, hell, if I'm going to live, I can use that stuff.

GATES: You'd better hurry, Duke. You don't want to miss the boat.

TAYLOR: *(Stands for a moment torn between his desire to leave and his desire for the suitcase. Then he dashes up the stairs)* Tell them to wait. I'll be right there.

GATES: *(Watching him)* I wonder if Duke will ever die. Why a man who has so little to live for should cling so hard to life . . . . People are a puzzle, Mrs. Clyme. People are a puzzle.

CLYME: I think it all came out rather well, don't you, Mr. Gates?

GATES: Yes, I think so. Of course, three are left.

CLYME: I don't mind abandoning *that* man.

GATES: No, I agree it doesn't make any difference about Taylor. I was thinking about the women.

CLYME: They had their chance.

GATES: True. They did. But all the same I rather liked Mrs. Allen. I thought you did, too.

CLYME: She wasn't at all what she seemed to be. She'll go back to her husband. She will, I just know it. She's common.

TAYLOR comes running down the stairs again, carrying his suitcase. He barely slows down to bid them good-bye.

TAYLOR: I ain't saying I had a good time, but I'm glad it's over.

GATES: If we had let Jenkins kill him, things might have been better.

CLYME: There's no sense looking back now. It's all over.

GATES: This time it's all over.

CLYME: Have you thought about the next group?

She goes to the French doors, closes them, and pulls the drapes. The stage grows dim.

GATES: Some.

CLYME: You're not ready to talk about it yet?

GATES: We might as well wait for the others.

> *The upstage door opens, and DONNE enters. He is followed by JENKINS and ROGERS. They are both dressed in the same style— black suits, white shirts, and black ties. A long red scar runs across Rogers' face. JENKINS has a large black spot on the side of his head. They are followed by MISS GRANT, now dressed like Mrs. Clyme. She wears dark glasses and carries a cane. They enter the room and stand in a row in front of the upstage center sofa.*

GATES: Sit down.

> *All but DONNE sit in mechanical fashion, staring straight ahead.*

CLYME: Where is Miss Britt? I thought I would make her my assistant.

DONNE: She should be coming with Mute.

> *MUTE enters alone and closes the door behind him.*

GATES: Where is Miss Britt?

DONNE: *(Looking at MUTE who looks at him)* She won't be coming.

GATES: What do you mean she won't be coming? *(To MUTE)* You fool, what have you done?

DONNE: Mute had nothing to do with it. She's made it. She hated no one even at the last moment.

GATES: *(Turning to MRS. CLYME)* That's what comes of your meddling, Mrs. Clyme.

GRANT: It wouldn't have made any difference. She didn't know how to hate. I was afraid of that.

GATES: Well ... those are the rules. I don't like missing one like this. But we are bound by the rules. I suppose I should be grateful I got Rogers. *(He walks downstage left, looks out)* It's going to be clear today. It will be nice for their traveling home. I wonder if we will ever see them again.

JENKINS: Taylor. Taylor, we'll see him again.

GATES: I'm afraid not, Jenkins. If you had moved faster, we'd have had him now. But I'm afraid we'll never see Taylor again.

CLYME: What about the next group?

GATES: This time I have a better plan. No Agatha Christie, this time. I thought perhaps we might go to some average town, say a place like *(Gives name of the city and stage in which the play is presented)* We could collect all our specimens in one place.

CLYME: *(Walking downstage toward him)* That should be easy. They have nothing but lonely people there, I've heard.

GATES: *(Moving toward the stage center and looking out over the audience)* We'll hire some hack to write a play about lonely people — we'll get the word *lonely* in the title. That will bring them out. Then we'll have our agents in the audience — Miss Grant, Jenkins, Rogers, Mute, Donne — something for everyone, the blind, the dumb, the halt, the sad. The lonely.

CLYME: I think our next group will be just lovely.

GATES: Yes, and we won't have to explain things to them. They'll see it all in the play — and they'll know we're waiting for them. Outside in the dark. *(Fast black out)*

FINAL CURTAIN